Happy Birthday 1983

3-1
7-30
7-8

Cowboy Riding Country

Cowboy Riding Country

John L. Sinclair

Illustrated by Edmond DeLavy

University of New Mexico Press
Albuquerque

© 1982 by John L. Sinclair. All rights reserved.
Jacket and illustrations by Edmond DeLavy.
Manufactured in the United States of America
Library of Congress Catalog Card Number 82-16089
International Standard Book Number 0-8263-0645-4
First edition
Design by Barbara Jellow

Sinclair, John L., 1902–
   Cowboy riding country.
     1. Ranch life—New Mexico.   2. Cowboys—New Mexico.
3. New Mexico—Social life and customs.   4. Sinclair,
John L., 1902–   I. Title.
F801.S585   1982   978.9′05   82-16089
ISBN 0-8263-0645-4

*To the Memory of
Stumpy Lucas
A Cowboy*

Shamrock Public Library

Contents

1	Where the Cowboys Hunkered Down	1
2	Jinglebob Town	13
3	Amonett's Saddle Shop	23
4	Rio Bonito	29
5	The Block Ranch	43
6	The Paterson Place	61
7	A Friendship With Casimiro	83
8	Cowboy Riding Christmas	91
9	Song of the Saddlemen	101
10	Bad From the Boots Up	109
11	The Sugarloaf Mountains	133
12	The Ghost Girl of the Mimbres	143
13	The Last Narrow Shave	151
14	The Rawhiders	163
15	Packhorse to Plumb Paradise	171
16	Light on Dark Mountain	181

One
Where the Cowboys Hunkered Down

Roswell, fifty years ago and more, was a valley oasis in the mighty expanse of grassy range cut from north to south by the Pecos River. And it was one of the greatest cow towns of them all.

The last time I saw Roswell was in 1942, when its population was less than fifteen thousand. Since then it has grown to nearly forty-five thousand—and cities of that size set my nerves on edge. I'd like to see Roswell again, but for the present I'll go there only in memory, when it had a comfortable population of seven thousand souls.

I knew it first in 1923, at the age of twenty, when I was staggered by its far-reaching latitudes, and by its abounding sunshine—having recently come from Scotland—a country where cloud and rain shut out a weak sun, and whose terrain is one of the most corrugated in the world.

The lightness of air impressed me most, unpolluted, circulating through the clean town. Concrete was everywhere along Main Street, very wide, running north to south. Sturdy buildings made a solid wall on either side, except where First, Second, Third, and Fourth Streets crossed the section that was the hub of town. Sprinklers kept the park surrounding the Chaves county courthouse carpeted with dense green turf. And what a balm of freshness there was where clear water met the grass! The same sweet scent that rises off the earth after a summer rain.

Roswell was the metropolis of all southeastern New Mexico, the source of supply for irrigated farms in the valley, and for ranches large and small in the radius of a hundred miles. Folks came north by dirt or graveled roads, up from valley communities, farmers mostly. But east, north, and west lay the rangelands—the domain of horseback men and gallant women, of cattlemen and cowboys, of sheepmen—whose lives and livings were concerned with grasslands measured by the square mile, not by the acre. Whether a man was a forty-dollar-a-month hand or the owner-manager of a 400-section barony, he was in the range-cattle industry, a member of a strong, quiet, clannish lot.

By the 1920s the frontier had passed into history, but its remnants lingered on the sea of grass that surrounded Roswell, and was especially felt on Roswell's most special corner.

The very center of the cowboy's world was the southwest quadrant of the corner on Main Street where Second crosses from east to west. It is a short strip of sun-bleached concrete, curbed and graced by a fire hydrant, one specially made to fit a hunkered-down cowboy's back. And it is forever hallowed in my memory as the spot where the cowboys met, where they joshed or made serious decisions, where they rolled a cigarette and hunkered down, as I did myself a half-century ago.

Right there at the corner were the places of business catering to cowboys' needs: Jay Duval's men's clothing emporium, the Smokehouse and Domino Parlor, and, up a flight of stairs, the Capitan Hotel. But the most patronized place was Katy's Cafe, where coffee was always on tap at five cents a cup. Katy's was a haven for rest and discussion, no booths or tables but a long center counter with stools where a feller could *really* hang his legs. The aroma that penetrated to the street was a truly delicious breath of the most wholesome and satisfying foods. A full-size dinner cost thirty-five cents. For slightly more you could get a steak cooked to perfection—about half the size of a saddle blanket.

Katy, by the way, was not a woman. He was big and masculine, with a manly voice. He was a restaurateur made to match the time and place, and the calibre of his not-so-dainty diners. He earned his "Katy" by having once been employed by the Missouri, Kansas & Texas Railroad.

Once, when entering the cafe, I met a bowlegged, sun-tanned, squinteyed customer on his way out. He had a satisfied look and plied a toothpick (an after-dinner exercise popular in Texas). He nudged me, spoke close to my ear, and with a friendly wink said, "Here's a tip: try the brains and eggs. Take it from me, they're *truly* delicious." I had no need to consult a menu that evening.

Katy, of course, didn't have one. His bill of fare was a blackboard, the items and prices listed in chalk. One offering was Fish—35¢. It might be fillet of sole, or more likely catfish, but at Katy's it was just plain Fish. Anything more descriptive would be *foofaraw*—as having a menu would be. And foofaraw was a despicable word in the cowboy tongue. It meant "puttin' on the dog" or "showin' off"—in short, pretentiousness.

There was no foofaraw about the cowboy character. A mere hint of it would alienate a man from the fraternal assembly at Second and Main. Any doodads in dress, the kind popularized by Hollywood, would brand the offender and the sight of him make a genuine working cowboy blush. The uniform of the range in the 1920s was black boots of shop-made quality, plain everyday khaki pants and a blue cotton shirt (the kind bought at J. C. Penney's north along Main), and none other than a genuine Stetson hat.

There were two moving picture theaters on Main Street, both operated by a man named Trieb. On the east side was the Princess, which exhibited "fancy pictures," or "that love stuff." Nothing like that went with Second and Main. Directly opposite the Princess was the Capitan, which offered Westerns—Tom Mix, Hoot Gibson, and William S. Hart. In spite of the phony treatment of ranch life, Westerns were preferable to love stuff. Most appreciated were the horses—and the way the professor banged the piano when the cattle stampeded.

A feller made an inquiry to me one Saturday afternoon, when we were both hunkered down near the fire hydrant:

> *The Feller*: You reckon Hoot Gibson will be in town this evenin'?
> *Me*: I don't know. If he is, you'll find him at the Capitan.
> *The Feller*: I reckon so. You just cain't keep old Hoot outa Roswell on a Saturday night.

But wait, old Hoot might have been popular on the silent screen, but just let him arrive to mingle with the bunch at Second and Main—him all rigged out in his Hollywood regalia. What do you reckon the bunch would have said? They'd have said nothing. They'd have just blushed, turned on their bootheels, and politely walked away. They just couldn't stomach foofaraw.

Because Second and Main catered to very special gentlemen's needs, there was a barbershop adjacent to the Smokehouse, with bathtubs and towels for rent in the rear. Lord, what a blessing! The works could be bought for one dollar—haircut fifty cents, shave twenty-five cents, bath twenty-five cents. When a man stays out on the grass for six weeks, never looking inside a town, mixing with horse sweat, absorbing bovine odors, and whiling away

his idle hours in a bunkhouse (sometimes an unsavory domicile itself), he's plumb-rarin' to get curried and dipped. Needless to say, the barber did a land-office business.

It's hard to guess what segment of the Second and Main congress patronized Emma's place at the corner of First and Virginia. But certainly it was the younger or middle-aged, transient hired cowhand element. Though Emma was not a part of Second and Main, she certainly was an institution. Some of the fellers gathered around the Smokehouse liked institutions, others didn't, the latter being husbands and such, solid citizens who had families of their own. Nonetheless, traffic to the perfumed destination was sometimes heavy.

If the word could be trusted, Emma was one of those with a heart of gold, who gave lavishly to charities, took in and nursed sick and friendless cowboys, contributed to the welfare and education of distant orphans, and behaved most generously in everything she did. Her girls were the best groomed and most ladylike of any west of Amarillo. There was no talk of her extending credit, however.

What was it that made Second and Main so urgent to the cowboy-cattleman's need for convention?

Well, it was central, for one thing: you could see the four horizons over the low rooftops, no buildings being more than two-story in height. The Bankhead Hotel, the stockman's favorite, was just down the block. Across the street was the Mabie-Lowery Hardware and the great wholesale house of Joyce-Pruitt was around the corner. Lee Crane, in from Diamond A headquarters, was everlastingly loading his Model T truck at the Joyce-Pruitt dock.

North, at the corner of Third, was the First National Bank, where ranch hands cashed their paychecks and the stockmen came pleading. Amonett's saddle shop was halfway down the block, where the smell of leather wafted out to the sidewalk, and the craftsmen within knew exactly what the boys at the corner preferred. Their customers were the most discriminating on earth. Saddle blankets were stacked like cordwood. Hanging from the wall were bridles, hackamores, ropes, chaps, reins, quirts, billets, and latigos, and within glassed cases glistened Crockett and Kelly bits and spurs, some silver-mounted. Quality was the name for the Amonett saddle, and rows of the product were on display.

Down the block was Kipling's Confectionary and Fountain. On television and the silver screen you've watched sons of the range quaff shot after shot of raw whiskey in sleazy saloons, but have you ever glimpsed a row of them, recently in from off the grass, discussing things that concerned them over ice cream sodas and banana splits? Prohibition was the law, and bootleg stuff could be readily bought, but never did I see the effect of red-eye at the corner of Second and Main. Never a brawl, never a drunken show of aggression. In fact, the ranch folk, most with roots in the Texas Bible Belt, were celebrated for church going, as witness the Cowboy Camp Meeting still held annually at Nogal Lake west of Roswell.

To Bankhead Hotel and Katy's Cafe, to the corner of Second and Main, came the established men of the grama grass sweep, the canyons and foothills, the creeks and baldies—from beyond the Caprock, from along the base of the Capitans.

They stood in groups, single or in pairs—dressed plain, giving out plain talk—or hunkered down with their shirttails out. Some were solemn, their minds on serious business, others laughed and joshed and cut up for the hell of it. Some were possessed of an original sense of humor, others repeated the same old guffaw-provoking cowboy platitudes, over and over again. Their serious talk and joshings concerned their one and only interest—the yellowed or greened-up flatlands and the human and animal lives thereon—and the elements that sent rain from heaven on the arid, thirsty ranges.

"You-all had any rain out at you-all's?"

"That old horse, he's gentle as a dog . . . And *action*, boy haddy! . . . I'm askin' twenty dollars for him. You bet, the price is high, but he ain't a cheap horse. I broke him out myse'f, he's got plenty cow-sense." (That's right, you could buy a good horse for twenty dollars back then.)

"That old boy, he got that old cow by the tail, and he *tweested* her down." (That bit of history always brought on the laughs.)

Conversation was serious business at Second and Main. Talkers talked quietly and listeners responded courteously, because the language used was a special one indeed. And when there was nothing more to say, each speaker turned away—without a "So long" or "I'll be seeing you." To say or do otherwise would be foofaraw.

Who's that old gentleman in the gray business suit, with white hair under a small Stetson hat, and a highly tanned face and white mustache, with keen squinted eyes and worn-out cigar—that old gent talking sense with a half-dozen cattlemen? Why, that's Captain Burton C. Mossman, general manager of the Bloom Land & Cattle Company's Diamond A Ranch, the big

8   Chapter One

outfit west of town and extending out into Lincoln County. "Cap" has an office upstairs of the First National Bank and the Diamond A regularly sends its delegates to the congregation in front of Katy's Cafe.

If you'd been around then and knew old Roger Hill, you'd have admired his saddle, bridle, and chaps—like all his cowboy leather gear, how they shone healthy with a constant dressing of oil. And what kind of oil, you reckon? It was extra-special lubricant, and potent, because Roger would ride out to the high-lonesome flats and catch the biggest diamondback rattlesnakes he could find—big fat rusty ones—and he'd take them to camp and boil them down and render the oil. That's why Roger Hill had the best saddle gear in Lincoln and Chaves counties. He never used cowboy boots, because he liked tennis shoes better, but he wore the biggest hat in the counties.

A Diamond A man in from the high baldies was Sam Butler, who in the heyday of The Corner was a man in his fifties. Some claimed he was an Englishman. He could have well passed for one. He had the clipped speech of the late H. V. Kaltenborn and his voice was quiet. He never failed to render good sense. And the glint in his eye was there to match his words. When he dealt out diction, he meant to be understood.

There was nothing English about Sam, however, except for the name of the town where he was born—Oxford, Mississippi. He came to Second and Main at regular intervals from his home at Crow Flat on the Diamond A, where he ran a bunch of fine mares and a few jacks, branded Rafter S, and from them raised mules of super quality. The saddle had bowed his legs, and the June wind had crackled his face to a rawhide texture.

Sam had a passionate affection for all children everywhere, and every spare minute he could afford he gave to their welfare and enjoyment. In Dexter, south of Roswell, Sam was especially loved, and once he was heard to say, "They manufacture some mighty fine kids down there."

But Sam used to like to josh about the younger generation, too, especially when he faced the street by the entrance to Katy's Cafe, or at the curb by the fire hydrant, chewing on a stogie waiting for victims. His prey was the male youth of the valley and plains, whom he referred to as buttons. Always with a twinkle, Sam didn't pack a lick of use for any young man under twenty-six. He'd say outright that that kind of feller was a disaster. He'd grab the shirt collar of some passing whipster of salad years, hold him firm and snap at the startled face, "They tell me you're a good button. Now you tell me this, what the hell good is a good button good for?"

But it was all in *hooraw*, all in fun.

Down from the north, from Yellow Lake and the Kenna vicinity, came the Crosbys—Mr. Crosby, Senior, a gentleman with poise and understanding, was one of the ablest cowmen to be found in the American West. And his son, Harold. And Bob, the rodeo champion, of whom it was said there wasn't a bone in his body that hadn't been broken.

And from way down in the opposite direction, from the Diamond A sheep headquarters at Walnut, not too far west of Artesia, came Charlie Corn. History has it that there lived in Roswell, down by the stageline station, in 1880, a man named Martin V. Corn. That was about the time they labeled the new town after the postmaster's father Roswell Smith. But they'd better have called it Cornville, or Cornstown, because Roswell was no more than a giant hub, and out of this hub sprouted spokes, and at the end of each was a ranch owned and operated by a master stockman surnamed Corn.

Now the Corn ranches are everywhere—far west into Lincoln county, north on the Macho at Eden Valley, and yonder toward the sunrise, anywhere that cattle graze the grama grass flats.

Then came the Block Ranch wagon cook, one Tom Weldy—chef extraordinary, philosopher, sage, man of thought and useful deed, and one of the most genuine, natural, poker-faced comedians ever to engineer the skillets under a potrack.

It's been said of Tom that he didn't like the nesters who were taking up homestead claims all over Block territory, ruining the grass, messing up the scenery, and starving themselves in the process. And he didn't like the way word got around to them every time he and the boys butchered a beef when the wagon was out—good meat for working cowboys on a roundup camp. When stew simmered on the potrack, complete with onions and all, and steaks fried in the skillets on the scrub-oak coals and sourdough biscuits baked in dutch ovens, the fragrance wafted over the grass to the claimshacks. Homesteaders were blessed with good noses.

One day, way back, a "sonovabitch" stew bubbled in the coals of Tom's campfire—the stew supreme, full of guts and fat. Brown chunks of beef, cooked to perfection, were stacked high in a tub, fried potatoes by the bucketful, pinto beans and rice-and-raisins—a plentiful supply, because Tom was prepared for the inevitable. A cowboy rode into camp from the roundup, hitched his pony to the wagon wheel and walked to the chuck box where Tom mixed up a batch of sourdough.

"By golly, Tom," that cowboy said enthusiastically, "it looks to me like we're havin' a sonovabitch for supper!"

Tom's eyes were focused on the wide-open flats, where down from the skyline a parade of nesters' wagons, loaded with families, was on the way.

"It looks to me like we're havin' about thirty of 'em," said Tom, and he meant every word of it.

There was another figure, aged but athletic—a man who possessed the respect of everyone gathered on that street corner. Black hat, the skirts of his black coat almost to his knees, and his black face aglow with the honesty and brightness of his nature—the last living spark of the initial cattle drive into southern New Mexico, that which stocked the plains and started it all. In 1867 when John S. Chisum drove ten thousand head of cattle out of Texas and established his "Long Rail and Jinglebob" brand on ranches at Fort Stanton, Bosque Grande, and Black River—with headquarters at South Spring, six miles south of Roswell—Uncle Frank Chisum—the offspring of slaves and then a small boy, rode behind the cantle of the Cattle King's saddle on that long historic drive.

The old-time bunch on the corner were people—therefore not paragons of what a man should be. Not perfect. There were the good and bad among them, the wise and the silly. Some were too human for their own good. Others packed no spark of humanity at all. It was a philosopher of their own kind—a Texas cowman—who claimed that if the human race could be divided into units of a hundred souls, each unit would contain one saint, one sonovabitch, and ninety-eight sheep.

Where are they now, that bunch?

They live on, in memory.

Look, the Block wagon is out, and Tom Weldy is summing up the nation's woes while he tends his potrack somewhere out yonder between White Flat and the Macho, piling scrub-oak coals on a dutch oven full of sourdough biscuits, thinking how if he were president in place of Calvin Coolidge he'd put the nation straight. . . . There, the horse wranglers are holding the *remuda*, a hundred head of all colors and dispositions. The cowboys are branding the roped calves pulled up to the fire, fussy little critters for the flankers to flank to the ground. They are out on the high lonesome and the nearest branding chute is at headquarters. The irons are reddening on a wood fire, hot as hell itself, in flame made of scrub oak and juniper, nothing so *foofaraw* as propane. . . . Riders are combing the pasture for more cattle. Horseback men on cutting horses are percolating their expert qualities—two sets of brains working as one, trotting into the herd and singling out the stuff to be worked. Boss and hands are hard at work, sweating in the dust, cussing a little, shouting and whistling a lot, thinking fondly of Tom Weldy's potrack, of Arbuckle's coffee and bacon and beans, of a mess of rice-and-raisins. Because dinnertime will come around, as sure as noon and midnight.

A trail herd is coming down off the Caprock, a couple hundred head of beef cattle bound for Roswell's Riverside shipping pens by the Santa Fe tracks. They trail out, the herd of them, mounted cowboys in the lead, the flanks and the drag. There's a *remuda*, and a chuck wagon, and a cook with a most cantankerous disposition. They'll get to Riverside tomorrow, but tonight they'll bed down the herd for one last feed of range grass before loading onto the cars, Kansas City–bound.

They've gone, the pioneers, the most of them. They've taken the old high-cantled, square-skirted, double-rigged saddle with them, and the little Spanish cow pony, popular at the time when the quarter horse was unknown. And the diamond hitch, and the wooden-towered windmill, and the spur on the boot that packed three-inch spiked rowels.

But they live on, each in his own eternity—his horse, his cattle, his pastures, and himself. And the way he stood at the corner of Second and Main, talking the same language to men whose thoughts were the same. "*You-all had any rain out at you-all's?*" . . . . "*Try the brains and eggs at Katy's, they're truly delicious.*" . . . . "*That old horse, he's gentle as a dog . . . .*"

Ride, cowboy, ride—forever and forever. You'll throw the diamond hitch, rope 'em down with the tied lariat, and carry the Texas talk of southeastern New Mexico even to the vapors beyond. Your eternity will be without foofaraw. And your heaven a wide grassy plain.

Two
Jinglebob Town

Many centuries ago, on a morning when the mists hung over the moor of Strathglas, the chief of Clan Chisholm called a conclave on a hilltop near his mountain stronghold. He gathered the clansmen of his name, his chieftains, and his piper, and proclaimed to Scotland and the Isles that from that moment on only *three* persons in all the world would qualify for the dignity of "The" before their names—The King, The Pope, and The Chisholm—equals all. He was behaving as one of his kind, for the clan chiefs of Scotland were celebrated for a severe lack of humility.

Little more than a century ago, a probable descendant of that mist-shrouded gathering was driving a herd of ten thousand cattle westward out of Texas, bound for the Pecos River valley where he would ultimately reign over a domain of his own and be hailed throughout the Southwest as *The Cattle King of New Mexico.*

He was John Simpson Chisum, the surname having been Americanized perhaps in the highlands of Appalachia sometime, since a Chisholm ancestor sought the freedom of America a century or so before. And the castle he would build was South Spring Ranch, about six miles south of Roswell, a fitting center of a cattle empire.

During the Civil War, Confederate Texans occupied themselves with the bayonet and rifle rather than with lariat and branding iron. As a result, vast herds of Longhorn cattle proliferated on the grasslands, unattended and unclaimed. Immediately on the restoration of peace, the Union military forces in New Mexico recognized that soon long wagon trains of settlers would be moving into the territory and ranches established and valley land broken to field wherever irrigation was obtainable. Prosperity won of hard work and enterprise was the promise New Mexico offered the strong and venturesome, together with peace of mind necessary for building home and fireside.

But there was one menace that threatened the hopes of all—the Indians, hostiles such as the Apache and Navajo. For that reason the military selected strategic sites for building forts in the Indian country, chief of these being Fort Stanton in the Mescalero Apache area and Fort Wingate where the Navajo exhibited a pugnacious spirit. Reservations with definite boundaries were laid out in the vicinity of the forts and government agencies installed to care for primitives who couldn't have cared less for the virtues of the white man's way of life. In spite of the cavalry presence, the Apaches and Navajos applied the paint and took off on the warpath. Settlers died as a result, had their livestock stolen and their homes burned. Fear of a "pueblo" life-style and forced Christianity fired both nomadic tribes to inflict terror on the white usurpers.

To force the "hostiles" to submission an area in the vicinity of old Fort Sumner was allotted to the military in 1864, called the Bosque Redondo (Spanish for *round grove of trees*). Here both tribes would be given a forced taste of civilization, after being rounded up and taken from their tribal ranges. The place of captivity was selected by Gen. James H. Carleton, but the cavalryman who engineered the actual roundup was Col. Kit Carson. Seven thousand Navajos—men, women and children—were herded like cattle to the Bosque Redondo, while a lesser number of Mescalero Apaches joined them for the hopeless experiment. The event is remembered by the Navajo as "The Long Walk."

On the Bosque Redondo, it was intended, warriors would be taught the industries of peace and so benefit from the day-long, year-long, life-long brow-sweat in agriculture, nineteenth-century mechanics, and the ways of a society alien to the total freedom of desert nomads. The experiment lasted four years and terminated in failure. In 1868, the government returned the Navajo to their former homes.

But seven thousand people held on a government reservation must be fed as they learn, and an Indian nomad's essential diet is composed of meat, accompanied by bread in a lesser amount. So contracts for the supply of beef in huge quantities were offered cattlemen whose nearest ranges were in Texas. Wild unbranded bovines swarmed the Texas grasslands, available for ear-marking and branding by anyone with the skill to capture them. In 1866 Charles Goodnight, initial settler and cattleman in the Panhandle, trailed a large herd to the Bosque Redondo to fill the first of the contracts.

His route was to the Horsehead Crossing of the Pecos, below present Carlsbad, then along the river's west bank northward. At the same time Oliver Loving, an elder Texas cattleman, tough as the Longhorns he gathered, was on the trail to honor another contract. He met with Goodnight and they formed a partnership, which was not to last. In a later drive Loving was killed in a fight with Comanches near the site of the present town of Loving named in his honor, but their venture has gone down in history as the Goodnight-Loving Trail. Together they were the precursors of trail driving into New Mexico.

Then came *The* Cattle King—*The* Chisum.

Like most pioneers, Claiborne and Lucinda Chisum raised a large family back in Madison County, Tennessee. August 15, 1824, a son John was born. Claiborne was a farmer and he raised all his children to be farmers. Madison county was lush between the south and middle forks that emptied into the Mississippi some sixty miles west. After Lucinda died, Claiborne remarried and moved his family to Texas, to settle on Mud Creek up against the town of Paris. Young John was thirteen.

In early manhood John Chisum ran for county clerk. He won, but days of confinement were not for him. After the Civil War, he engaged in the cattle business. He yearned for the wide horizons, the freedom, and the constant movement that trailing the Longhorns offered. He drove three small herds to a packing house in Little Rock, which proved a disaster and plunged him into bankruptcy. He claimed that his only assets were the wild Texas cattle, unbranded and of no cash value, so the judgments against him became worthless scraps of paper.

During the war he supplied the Confederate army with beef cattle at forty dollars a head, and used the money to purchase land and horses. His first ranch was in Denton county. (He later claimed that the site of Fort Worth was on his range.) His next venture was at Fort Concho, not far from present San Angelo, which gave him his first leg of the journey into the western hinterland. Besides his cattle interests, John Chisum served as a store clerk in a town northeast of his ranch, working himself into a partnership. There he learned of new opportunities from a relative who had fled Texas for New Mexico after killing a man—"on the dodge" as the cowboy term defines it.

Tol Chisum had returned to Texas for trial and been pardoned. He told John of the great opportunities open for supplying beef cattle on government contract to the Indians at the Bosque Redondo. He described with enthusiasm the nature of the Pecos country, a true cattleman's paradise.

So in the year 1867, a historic one for Roswell and its cowboy riding country, John Chisum gathered cowboys and drove his first herd into New Mexico. His route led over the Texas plains, across the Llano Estacado, to follow the Goodnight Trail to the Horsehead Crossing of the Pecos and terminate the drive at the Bosque Grande. This was a choice site for a ranch about thirty miles down river from Fort Sumner, the thick black grama grass knee-high to a horse. Grama is the most nutritious range feed in the West, and at Bosque Redondo there were thousands upon thousands of acres of it.

Chisum's first trail herd numbered six hundred head. He sold it to the military, and was rewarded with a contract to supply another ten thousand. He filled the order by rounding up Texas Longhorns and branding them with his own special mark—"The Long Rail"—a burn of distinction starting behind the animal's left shoulder in one straight line hindward across the "ribs." The earmark called a *Jinglebob* was accomplished by making a slip on both ears, causing one part to flip downward while the other remained in its natural position. Quick identification of Chisum cattle could be made by the earmark alone.

Chisum was an old hand at the cattle drive. The year before the long trail that made New Mexico his permanent home he had supplied Honeywell, Kansas, with cattle from Brown County, Texas. On filling his contract for the second big cattle drive from Texas, Chisum established a ranch at the Bosque Grande. The Apaches and Navajos were returned to huge land allotments on their old tribal ranges, but the Cattle King continued buying stock on the hoof in Texas and selling it at a profit to Fort Sumner for supplying the reservations.

The Bosque Grande was a beautiful dream come true for any cattleman whose idea of heaven was grass, water, winter shelter, and a hundred other benefits that make for successful ranching. But he had lost his heart to another location, one south of Bosque Grande by thirty-seven miles. In fact, it was absolutely the one truly ideal landscape within the horizons of human, equine, and bovine habitation. It was where the Rio Hondo flowed down from Sierra Blanca (White Mountains) westward some eighty miles to combine its waters as a tributary of the Pecos. In the same vicinity were two other streams, both to empty into the Hondo before it merged with the Pecos—the North Spring and South Spring rivers. In 1874, at South Spring, Chisum bought a tract of land suitable for headquarters and here established his permanent home. South Spring Ranch was an estate destined to become famous throughout the cowboy West, a short six miles south of where the city of Roswell is today.

It was in 1882 that John Chisum built the "Long House" that would become a fit castle for his cattle kingdom. In all eastern New Mexico and west Texas there was no other spread to compare with his South Spring Ranch. Its extensive fields, orchards, gardens, and fenced pastures were irrigated by a vast canal and ditch system fed by artesian wells.

The Long House was of adobe, containing nine rooms of the same size in a single row, with *galleries*, or porches, running the entire length on either side. (There was a room for the dances held frequently, for Chisum was a fiddler of no small talent.)

A ditch stocked with fish ran under and across the house. The "King" amused himself and any of his staff or guests, by feeding the fish cracker crumbs. They became so tame they would bite at the offering held under water by hand. Housekeepers maintained The Long House and supervised the staff. House furnishings were comfortable and in good taste, but in spite of the luxury they provided, Chisum refused the comfort of bed and mattress. He slept on soogans (quilts) and blankets laid flat on the floor, with probably a rolled-up saddle blanket for a pillow. He was the greatest of cattlemen, but at heart he was a *cowboy*—as much a cowboy as any of the "bunch in the bunkhouse."

Between 1870 and 1881, Chisum is said to have had the largest cattle holdings in the world, with range extending from the original Bosque Grande Ranch at the north to a south boundary on the Texas line, a distance of one hundred fifty miles. The site of the present city of Carlsbad was a Chisum cowcamp. He maintained a ranch at Fort Stanton that filled government beef contracts to supply the Mescalero Apaches. He even supplied cattle for beef to the San Carlos Apache reservation in Arizona. Outpost ranches were at Seven Rivers, Black River, and camps far out on the eastside plains beyond the Caprock. To west of the Pecos his cattle and horses, branded **U** on the left shoulder, grazed the arroyos and baldies east of the Capitans and the mighty sea of black grama grass north of the mountains.

It is estimated that in his heyday Chisum ran herds aggregating one hundred thousand head and employed a hundred fifty cowboys. He petitioned President Grant for a patent to cover the entire area, but was denied one. He nevertheless maintained his cattle kingdom, and the word was spread advising settlers to keep off. The West's most notorious outlaw, Billy the Kid, was at one time a Chisum cowboy, as were others of his gang. In 1878 Chisum became involved in the Lincoln County War, a feud between rival merchants in Lincoln. Outlaw and Indian depredations seriously reduced his cattle and horse herds.

John Chisum died in December, 1884. He left a legacy consisting of all manner of litigation that plagued the great ranch until 1893, when the Colorado empire-builder-railroad-tycoon, J. J. Hagerman, bought the holdings. In 1904 much remodeling was done, but Hagerman left the Long House intact. At a later time the South Spring section of the ranch was acquired by Cornell University where experiments in the scientific growing of range grasses and livestock fodder were carried on.

A ruin about twelve or fifteen miles up the Rio Hondo marks the site of the first settlement in the area where the city of Roswell was to be. It is known to residents as "Missouri Plaza." Not that the settlers were from Missouri, but rather they were Spanish Americans down from the old settlements adjacent to the Manzano mountains, specifically from the town of Manzano in present Torrance County. They built their adobe houses and laid out their fields, and they took water from the Hondo for irrigation. They arrived in 1866 or '67, about the time the cattle barons were trail-herding their cattle from Texas to the Bosque Redondo.

Why the "Missouri" is part of the name was for sometime a mystery. But now it is believed that, having come from the Manzano mountains, which is in the Albuquerque-Santa Fe area, the settlers were at times employed in the commerce of the Santa Fe Trail, and the eastern terminus of the great trade route had an affectionate significance for them. Their community lasted only a few years, for upstream irrigation in the Lincoln-Ruidoso valleys captured most of the Hondo's water and an insufficient flow was left for the Missouri Plaza fields. They packed up and left in 1872, probably joining Manzano Mountain kinsmen in the valleys to the west.

So with the drover barons out of Texas the cowboy riding country of New Mexico took shape and form—a form that was Texan in every respect: Texas talk and mores, Texas customs in dress, Texas taboos, Texas ideals in fundamentalist religion, Texas prudery and clannishness, and a Texas cattle industry.

There are towns today that seem like lighted seaports, harbor lights fronting a sea of grass. *Las Vegas*, New Mexico, for one, snug against New Mexico's highest mountains from which roads stretch out to the south and east and north, to grasslands surrounding islands of homes, stores, post offices—*Mosquero, Solano, Roy, Clayton, Logan, Tucumcari, Santa Rosa . . . Santa Fe*, southward to *Moriarty, Mountainair, Vaughn. . . . Socorro*, trading port of the San Augustin Plains, the Jornada del Muerto and the Continental Divide country merging into the Gila . . . *Carrizozo* of the Chupadera Mesa and Lincoln Forest highlands, of the Capitans and the rugged confines of the Bar W range—of the Oscuras, the mountains of darkness and obscurity . . . *Tularosa*, of old Pat Coghlan's Three Rivers Ranch, of Susan Barber, a latter-day "Cattle Queen" as John Chisum was "The King" of earlier times . . . *Alamogordo*, center of Circle Cross country, where Oliver Lee rode . . . *Deming*, center of the greasewood flats that rise to the cathedral spires of the Floridas, of the Columbus border where Pancho Villa messed up the town, to the Mimbres, to the copper treasure chest of Santa Rita . . . *Silver City*, where the desert rolls on to Arizona across the Burro mountains . . . *Lordsburg*, the night lights that glitter northward of the Animas, the San Simon, the once vast Diamond A empire . . . And lastly, *Roswell*—the Jinglebob Town that John Chisum pioneered.

The new county of Lincoln had been surveyed in 1866, an area covering all southeastern New Mexico and as large as five eastern states, the most extensive but sparsely populated county in the nation. A year later Hiram Fellows was surveying on a government contract in the region where Chisum's South Spring Ranch was soon to be, and had mapped off a few townships surrounding the confluence of the Rio Hondo and the greater Pecos. Contained in his survey was choice land situated between the South and North Spring Rivers. It was rich valley soil with an abundance of irrigation water available.

Several claims of 160 acres each were filed, one of which fell into the hands of Thomas Catron, the attorney, politician and mighty commercial tycoon of "Santa Fe Ring" notoriety. In 1870 a professional gambler, Van Smith, along with his father, Roswell Smith, acquired the Catron quarter section. There were a few homes in the district, little more than crudely built shacks beside irrigation ditches. Smith took a partner, Aaron Wilburn, and together they started a mercantile business, and named the village Rio Hondo. But the following year, when the business began to show promise, when Wilburn and three others filed quarter sections of land apiece, Smith had a post office located in the new town and the name changed to honor his father, Roswell. The land filings covered all of what is the business district of Roswell today.

Chisum prospered on his ranch, and the little town of Roswell grew as settlers moved into the area in spite of the cattle king's warning to would-be townbuilders to keep out. The Pecos Valley here was a bonanza of agricultural gold, and beyond for hundreds of miles in all directions range grasses flourished. In 1889 the Territorial Legislature carved a county of its own for Roswell, naming it to honor Colonel J. Francisco Chaves of a distinguished Spanish-American family and a pioneer of southeastern New Mexico.

In 1889, the Pecos Valley Irrigation and Investment Company began its great system of canals and ditches. Cattlemen trailed their foundation herds in from Texas, blocking up ranches on the flats and baldies from the Caprock to Picacho Hill—in every direction.

By 1900, Roswell had grown from a population of 343 to over 2,000, when J. J. Hagerman moved from Colorado to live on and improve John Chisum's old South Spring Ranch. Only six years earlier, along with partners Charles B. Eddy and others, Hagerman had laid track for the Pecos Valley Railroad, to complete the line north from Eddy (Carlsbad) to Roswell, but at the turn of the century, he extended it as the Pecos Valley & Northeastern to Amarillo, Texas. In 1901 this line was incorporated into the Belen Cutoff system of the Atchison, Topeka & Santa Fe.

Within two decades, Roswell established herself as the Queen City of southeastern New Mexico, and her Pecos Valley with its artesian wells and rows of cotton and corn, alfalfa and thriving orchards became a transplanted Eden. The irrigated land extended south a distance of sixty miles. Dexter, Hagerman, and Artesia were thriving towns along the way. They were farmer towns, cattleman towns, and the latter named became terribly involved in oil, with fields of the treasure over the great plains to the east. In the early day an unsuspecting settler drilled his water well too deep, and by that accident started the largest artesian-irrigated valley in North America. The wells range from four hundred to a thousand feet deep. In 1929 the most voluminous artesian well in the world was located nine miles southeast of Roswell, flowing nearly ten thousand gallons a minute.

There were almost two thousand acres in apple trees, more than twenty thousand acres in cotton producing two bales to the acre, thousands of acres of alfalfa cutting two tons to the acre, and three thousand acres in corn. Truck garden harvests and enormous yields of oats, sorghum, and miscellaneous crops brought the valley's total production to nearly $3 million.

A summer of abundant rainfall and a thick growth of grama grass, with enough humidity to give life and juice to the fruits of the soil, made 1929 a prosperous year for the brotherhood of drovers and herders, for husbandry of fields and orchards, for people of the sun who lived remote from industrial congestion as those who toiled and thrived in the faraway Pecos Valley.

Yet, as all the world knows, it was the year of disaster for Wall Street. By 1931, stock losses had risen to fifty billion dollars, and the Great Depression had set in.

But what about Tug, Ollie, and Matt Porter who ranched west of Roswell on Salt Creek? Those good old boys who raised fine Hat X brand whiteface cattle, gents noted and envied by cattlemen of the area for running their business with such remarkable efficiency that they never "slid into debt and always kept out of trouble?"

How did *they* suffer the Great Depression? Not much. They'd have liked their calves and yearlings to bring better prices in Kansas City, but so long as the grass made its normal growth, the cattle waxed fat, the horses ran slick and the larder held plenty of beans and bacon, a feller could stay in business. And come weekend nights crank up the flivver and take in the dances at Pine Lodge. Because as Tug once explained it to me, "I'm a dancing piece of furniture."

And what would Stumpy Lucas have to say about the Great Depression—old Stump, that "cowboyin' son of a gun!"—who had lived his sunny days for twenty years out at "Five," the Bloom Land & Cattle Company's main cowcamp, riding after Diamond A cattle, straddling Circle Diamond horses, earning forty dollars a month and chuck, a wage that stayed level, never went up or down, enough for any man on earth if he had a range to ride with the sun above, and the dry breeze against his face, on a cowpony with sense between his ears.

Ask Stumpy what he reckoned about the depression, or if he was hurt by inflation, or if he packed a fear of recession, and he would say, "Well hell! Where did you git them jawbustin' words?"

The farmers of the valley, the sheepmen of the flats and the Hondo hills, the cattlemen and their cowboys, all together built the town and put life and living between North and South Spring creeks. They made Main Street with its shops and banks and offices of the professionals, brilliant in sunlight by day, the wideness and cleanliness of it aglow with tastefully placed street lamps on the darkest of nights. There was no need of a park, for the entire residential section was a park—trim houses of cream-colored brick or substantially built frame, lawns in the shade of weeping willow and cottonwood, steeplelike Lombardy poplar.

The foundation stones of Roswell were laid not by John Chisum alone, but by Smith, Lea ("The Father of Roswell"), Chaves, Wilburn, Patterson, Hudson, Wildy, White, Miller, Upson, Otero, Cahoon, Dow, Lusk, Church, Amonett, Anderson, Ballard, Coe, Corn, Fresquez, Tomlinson, Dills, Farnsworth, Hinkle, Jones, Huffman. And Poe, and Garrett, and Mossman—three stern maintainers of law and order. These were the men who built the center of cowboy riding country.

Three
Amonett's Saddle Shop

When the cowboy of fifty years ago paid a visit to Roswell every few weeks for the purpose of rest and trade, first he'd call at the Smokehouse barbershop for a shave, haircut, and bath, then a steak and cornbread dinner at the cowboy corner cafe. And when he sought to buy a night of hospitality, he would often choose Aunt Kate's Rooming House—where cleanliness, decency, and kindness were items on the bill at seventy-five cents or a dollar at the most, a little costlier than rates at the upstairs hotels along Main Street but well worth the extra.

Then, down the block from the First National Bank, not too conspicuous when measured by its importance to life and work on the range, was the saddle, bridle, boots and spurs empire of E. T. Amonett and his son Edd, master craftsmen in leather, dealers in all the trappings of the man on horseback, whose speciality was the Western stock saddle, square- or round-skirted, double-rigged and high-cantled—the right match for the most intelligent, nimble, sometimes fractious of all equines, the cow pony.

I remember the fragrance of the place, the smell of rich quality leather that met one on entering the shop from the sun-brightened street. The entrance was awninged, as were all important show-window emporiums along that street, and in the gentle light samples of the merchandise were displayed in the window to whet the appetites of men whose livelihood and prosperity depended on the trappings that the Amonett Saddlery had to offer.

The Amonett saddle was recognized throughout the Southwest for its comfort. Match that quality with the easy, regular pace of the small well-trained Spanish pony, and the hours spent in pastures or on the trail seemed like minutes.

Chapter Three

They came, the cattlemen and sheepmen. They judged leather and horse trappings with the feeling hand and the gimlet eye. No patronage in the nation could be as demanding as theirs. And Edd Amonett, his saddle- and bootmakers, and his wife Nettie had riding the cattle range in their very blood—were born to it, their forebears lived by it, and the fussy patronage respected them for it.

The premises were long and narrow, with walls hung to the ceiling with merchandise, like chaps, (wide-winged and open at the seat to apron a cowboy's legs for the rough jobs in the saddle), bridles and breast collars, hackamores, reins, latigos, saddle strings and quirts, hobbles, stirrups and tapaderos, and cinches in cotton, fishcord, or mohair. Billets and bosals or nosebands. They were all there.

Also hanging in attractive coils were lariats in manila, linen, and maguey. The manila and linen lariats were smooth on the hands, and strong. Mexican maguey rope was light and easy to handle. Since it never became soft or saggy with use, held a loop better than any other, and was the most accurate rope for throwing, it was popular in stunt or fancy-roping contests and performances. For heavy work, like steer roping, however, the manila was the desired instrument.

At Amonett's, saddle blankets were stacked on a bench—Navajos, woven angoras, quilted hair pads, and wool mix (the kind guaranteed never to wrinkle under the saddle), and the Corona, the truly dress-up blanket, created to match a silver-mounted saddle, and supplied on special order.

Navajo saddle blankets were much in demand because of their durability and their harmony with the hand-stamped leather brown of a crafted stock saddle, such as an Amonett. They came in background colors of white or grey, with designs of black and red predominating, but they were all one-of-a-kind. They were sold by the pound—two dollars a pound—the singles averaging two to three pounds, thirty by thirty inches square. The doubles weighed four to seven pounds and measured thirty-four by fifty-six inches. They usually came in four grades, the finest suitable for choice floor rugs. At Amonett's the cowboy demanded the best, and he was certain that *there* he would get it.

The Amonetts carried boots made in the shop by Mat Brand himself. And spurs! how they shone in their glass cases! a spur for each heel to tickle that pony in the flanks, perk him into action, and ride a high lope hell-bent after that owl-head critter. So Edd Amonett would show his customer a pair stamped *Crockett*, proof that they are genuine, the best in the West; silver-mounted, maybe, with two-and-a-half inch rowels, possibly, tinkling their cathedral chimes when you walked.

But it was the Amonett saddle that drew the bowlegged patronage, the special customers whose pride was the leather perch of their daily lives—double-rigged by preference in the Southwest, round or square-skirted, with swell-forks anywhere from twelve to sixteen inches, size of seat to fit the individual rider, with cantle a traditional five inches in height; and horn riveted to the fork, showing bare polished metal, or leather or rawhide-covered—all parts of the sculpture in wood, the frame on which the saddle is built, called the *tree*. The side jockeys of it, the bronze or plated dees or rings, the latigos and billets, the stirrups and strings, the nickel conchas, the front and flank cinches which cowboys new from Texas called *girths*. The hand stamping in attractive designs, the clean sheepskin innerside that made contact with the horse—all in all the right saddle to fit a cowboy's horse, and above all the cowboy taste for good things made of leather.

Saddle makers of the Southwest built their saddles to suit the small Southwestern pony of Spanish-Barb or mustang origin. (Larger, heavier cow horses were favored in the Northwest.) A cowboy who ordered a saddle from the catalog of R. T. Frazier of Pueblo, Colorado, or out of Cheyenne or Miles City, would usually insist it be built on a *pony tree*. Edd Amonett, on the other hand, could size up a man at a glance, figure the kind of horse he would ride, and tailor the saddle to the rider.

At that time, the cost of a good saddle, from eighty to one hundred twenty dollars, would require every dime of two to three months of a cowboy's wages—maybe a year at putting aside ten dollars a month for the purpose, one-fourth of his forty dollars per. The working rider seldom rode a mare; the gelding was the partner in the day's work. Nor would he ride a "mail order" saddle. The Sears, Roebuck catalog for 1927 (and how we gloated over that 1100-page book!), offered stock saddles at various prices, the finest at $49.98. But I never heard of a cowboy in all Chaves or Lincoln counties who would stoop to throw a leg over any other than the product of a Western saddle maker who had the salty sweat and grueling hardships of the cowboy world in his veins.

Of course, it would take a different size saddle seat to fit scrawny Stumpy Lucas from the Diamond A—alkali-blistered, with legs out of proportion with the rest of his frame, which didn't matter, for he was only comfortable astride a horse. In contrast to huge Lee Corn, member of the magnificent

Corn Clan whose ranches stretched far and near from this cowboy hub. Edd Amonett could suit them all.

A characteristic of the ranch country is that the ablest of men seem to stay with good employers forever. Bill Wolf, an old friend of the Amonetts moved in from Corsicana in 1905, to remain with the shop until his death in 1939. Then, in 1929, Matt and Dorrell Brand, a married couple, joined the force. They were the bootmakers, he crafting the lower part, she stitching the upper. Again, the Brands worked for Edd Amonett until he retired in 1949, when they continued the business under the Amonett name. Matt died in 1974, and Dorrell kept the business going until she sold it in 1978. In all, the Brands were with the name Amonett for forty-five years.

In recent times, the pickup truck and horse trailer had come to stay and styles in saddlery changed to meet the tastes of a less salty, not so rugged younger generation. Expert leather stampers were hard to find. Rodeo contestants found it easier to stay on a pitching bronc if his saddle seat was made with the flesh-side out, rather than the slick handstamping. Calf ropers found it quicker and easier to get off the saddle if the cantle was lower—down to four inches, even lower. They asked for larger, leather or rawhide-covered horns, as the tied lariat was hard to keep fastened to the small metal ones. Professional athletes are setting a fashion in saddles, the new working cowboy accepting the trend. The old-time West was passing away, as the frontier West died with the nineteenth century.

Throughout its long lifetime, the Amonett shop catered mostly to the ranch, to the man whose business was beef or mutton and wool production. To those whose demands were practical. But many big names in Rodeo were patrons, too, boys with special needs, as well as breeders of show horses, who required exhibition saddle gear to garnish some of the finest horseflesh not for the sake of mere vanity, but an absolute necessity toward successful sales. Glitter and flash to dress up a California Palomino.

Several such orders were received, one from Leo V. Connell of Connorsville, Indiana, requesting a price on two riding outfits, saddles, Corona saddle blankets, bridles, and tapaderos, breast collars to match, hand-stamped and silver-mounted—one for himself, the other for his wife. The order was filled and the price for each was $3,500.

The most elaborate saddle made by the Amonetts was on order for B. M. Marshbank of Hanford, California, rancher and breeder of Palominos. The work was started March 23, and completed May 10, 1948. The finest of craftsmen took part in the project—Edd Amonett, himself; Ed Raymond, Andrew Tucker, Charles Brodie, and McCabe Raymond. Total time spent, 442 hours. The leather stamping was done by Andrew Tucker, silver fittings by Ed Raymond.

Seventy-eight square feet of leather was used on the job, which amounts to two-and-a-half cowhides. Thirty-two square feet of woolskin was required for the saddle and Corona blanket. Four sheep produced the woolskin required. Over ten pounds of silver were used. Three hundred and fifty-two pieces served as mountings on the saddle, bridle and breast collar. Thirty solid gold horseheads made up an overlay for the mountings. In the fifty years of the saddlery this was the finest saddle made—price to Mr. Marshbank, five thousand dollars.

After Edd Amonett retired, he purchased the Cree Meadows Golf Course at Ruidoso, operated for almost ten years, and divided his time between the mountain and valley cities. He died in 1963. Today, Nettie Amonett lives in the Amonett home on Gaye Drive—in Roswell's residential district, where spreading shade trees completely canopy the streets from side to side, distinguishing them as among the most beautiful in the Southwest. And in the peace and quiet of it all, she lives in memory with the days and events long passed on.

In her memories, she rides the pastures of Weed again, drinking the cool air of the high Sacramentos; she sits with the sway of the covered wagon on the trails down to the ranch near Elkins—hears the bawl of milling cattle as the Circle Y stuff are rounded up and brought in from the pastures. She talks the language of the range with the patrons of the saddle shop, in to buy a new saddle, a rope or a latigo, horseback folk from the Rio Feliz and Peñasco, from the Ruidoso and the pastures near Lincoln Town, some of the greatest cowboys in the heritage of New Mexico.

They live in Nettie Amonett's wealth of memories, now. In her living room is a miniature horse carved by her late daughter Jean, perfect as only the heart and hand of a horsewoman can carve it; and perfect, too, is the miniature saddle, full-stamped with leather-covered stirrups, matching tapaderos and mohair cinch, a memorial to the range times and range people that were.

Four
Rio Bonito

Some folks wouldn't call it a river at all. They'd call it a *creek* if they'd come from the South, a *brook* if the East was their place of origin. But they'd all agree that it's "pretty," which is the name the Spanish gave it a century-and-a-quarter ago: *Rio Bonito* (Pretty River).

It was named in 1855 when Spanish settlers from the Rio Grande Valley and the *ranchos* and *placitas* adjacent to the Manzano mountains arrived with their ox carts and herds to found a new and far more remote village of their own—one they named La Placita del Rio Bonito because of the trickle of a river that can convert to a torrent after a rain, and because of their ranchos up and down the narrow mountain valley. Then again and permanently named Lincoln, in honor of the president martyred after the dead of Gettysburg were under their grass.

The Bonito is pretty because it begins with drainage down from the 12,000-foot peak of Sierra Blanca, where rains seep and snows melt off the slopes of Nogal Peak and Loma Grande—where aspens quiver and pine and spruce, fir and hemlock, and the lovely balsam are alone with wildlife that populate the land. Where in season the meadows are rampant with blankets of black-eyed susans and yellow sunflowers, wild asters, and here and there an Indian Paintbrush, lush ferns in the shade of the forest, wild strawberries and raspberries, mushrooms and funguses that thrive in the damp—all to contribute to the Bonito, tumbling into Bonito Lake, a fisherman's paradise.

Downward and eastward the Rio Bonito flows through pine thickets and grassy meadows, to touch Lincoln Town before joining the *Rio Ruidoso* (Noisy River) to become the *Rio Hondo* (Deep River). About six miles upstream of Lincoln Town is Fort Stanton, once an important military post, established in 1855 to restrain the warlike Mescalero Apaches, then the most hostile Indians in New Mexico. At first Fort Stanton was a mere stockade surrounding shacks and corrals. This primitive installation was burned by its own Union troops when invading Confederate Texans from Fort Bliss advanced on them on August 2, 1861. A year later General James Carleton and his California Column rebuilt the garrison, much to the relief of settlers who had been harassed by Indians during the military absence.

After the Civil War, many troopers settled in the Bonito Valley to take up farming and ranching, or were lured into mining by the excitement at White Oaks, Nogal, Kraut Gulch, and the Black Range. But infantry and cavalry still occupied the fort until 1896 when it was converted to a hospital for the Merchant Marine at a time when New Mexico was celebrated for its curing powers on sufferers of tuberculosis. In 1953 the State of New Mexico took over the hospital facilities for the treatment of Indians, while other parts of the old fort provided quarters for the state's minimum security prisoners. Since then it has been used for various projects of the state government.

The naming of Fort Stanton carries a dramatic story of its own. Howard Bryan of the Albuquerque *Tribune*, probably the state's foremost nonacademic historian, and the most readable and entertaining, has it that on January 7, 1855, Captain Henry Whiting Stanton while scouting in the Sacramento Mountains with a hundred fifty troopers of the First Dragoons, was joined on the Rio Ruidoso by Captain Richard Ewell and eighty dragoons from Los Lunas. Stanton and Ewell moved south and on the night of January 18 made camp in a canyon near the site of present-day Mayhill.

They were surprised at sunrise by one hundred Mescalero Apache warriors on a hilltop ready to fight.

The Indians built a fire and danced around it, hurling insults at the troopers and daring them to fire a shot. The Apaches were outnumbered, but skirmished with the dragons throughout the day with no casualties on either side.

Late in the afternoon, when the Indians would soon be retiring from the fight due to the custom of no battle after dark, Captain Stanton and twelve of his men made their way into a canyon to meet the enemy from another direction. There they were ambushed and Stanton was killed instantly with a bullet to the head. His body, and that of a private who was also killed in the ambush, were buried that night on a spot nearby. Fires were kindled over the graves to obliterate their location. But four days later, when a squad of dragoons returned to the site, they found the graves had been ravaged, and the blankets stolen from the bodies. The soldiers built a pyre on which the flesh was burned, but the bones were retrieved and taken to Fort Fillmore. Captain Stanton's remains were given to his widow on February 16, twenty-three days after the killing.

Stanton's widow asked Governor Meriwether of New Mexico to retrieve if possible the sword, pistols and watch her husband was carrying when he was killed. At a peace conference in the Mesilla Valley in June of that year, Governor Meriwether talked with an Apache, Cuchillo, who claimed he was the brave who killed Captain Stanton. The governor showed his own personal watch and asked if Captain Stanton had one similar. The Indian nodded that he had, and,

"It kept talking all night, saying tick-tick-tick. Then it died and I buried it."

Cuchillo returned the watch to the military and it was sent to Mrs. Stanton.

But if the Rio Bonito is a life vein, Lincoln Town is the pulse, a throb that will beat for generations to come because of one reckless life-waster of a freckle-faced, buck-toothed tramp on horseback. Billy the Kid remains the idol of a fraternity of outlaw-doters, six-gun enthusiasts, fodder for the element that can abide to watch violence on television for hours on end. And to his shrine, although he is buried elsewhere, come an estimated 40,000 glorifiers annually.

In tune with pilgrim interest is an organization founded and financed by one of the wealthiest men in America, and certainly one ranking as the nation's top land buyer and owner—Robert O. Anderson and his Lincoln County Heritage Trust. Ever since the Old Lincoln County Courthouse Museum was opened to the public in May, 1940, as a branch of the Museum of New Mexico, the intent was to credit the law-abiding, pioneering ranchmen and farmers, merchants and all and sundry whose combined ambitions were to wipe out outlawry, civilize the nearby Apache Indians and provide rustic peace and quiet industry for nineteenth-century Lincoln county—then the largest county in the nation, with a land area equal to the states of Connecticut, Vermont, Delaware, Massachusetts, and Rhode Island combined. But it would be hard to find a pioneer of a hundred years ago, in the sparse population of so huge a territory, who hadn't in some way, just or unjust, been influenced by Billy the Kid and the Lincoln County War of 1878.

In Lincoln Town, today, is the large two-story adobe building with the white-painted balcony, the Old Lincoln County Courthouse, once the political pulse of the huge expanse of geography in the early 1880s, now a state museum. It was built in the 1870s as the commercial headquarters of the Murphy-Dolan Company—merchants and wielders of shady political influence. A short distance eastward down the street is the famous Tunstall-McSween store, also a state museum. Together with the "Big House," as the Murphy concern was called, made targets of each other in the feud of 1878. Billy the Kid, the folk hero of sorts, had much to do with both.

There is the old circular rock-walled Torreon, the fortified watch tower used by the earliest settlers for protection against the Indians. There is the Isaac Ellis house where Governor Lew Wallace conferred with Billy the Kid, offering the outlaw amnesty if he would halt his desperate ways. There is the rebuilt and state-owned Wortley Hotel, where bed and board of exquisite quality may be purchased; and Roman Maes's La Paloma Museum, not so long ago an historic saloon. The Heritage Trust has restored several old buildings such as the Montaño store of ancient vintage, the Luna house, the homes once occupied by the Gallegos and Chavez families, and the Doc Woods domicile, all financed out of the Anderson bank account, which is said to be as vast in figures today as Lincoln county was in acres a hundred years ago.

Billy the Kid was born in New York City on November 23, 1859. Little is known of his father except that he was Irish, and surnamed Bonney. His mother, Catherine Bonney, married a man named Antrim, after the Kid's actual father went into oblivion. Court records list the Kid as William H. Bonney, sometimes as William Antrim, other times as Henry McCarty.

Legend has it that Billy the Kid killed his first man in Silver City, New Mexico, in 1871. He would have been twelve years old. But another story gives the date of his first step into infamy as 1877, when he was a tougher eighteen. His victim was a blacksmith called Windy, and it happened in George Adkin's saloon, in Fort Grant, Arizona. Windy was a huge man, possessed of a loud mouth and a peculiar habit of bullying and beating up men smaller than himself. But one night, when for the pleasure of onlookers, he pinned to the floor and pummeled Billy the Kid, he invited to his stomach pit a slug from a .45—for a Colt of that calibre was a necessary part of the Kid's apparel. With Windy dead, the Kid ran from the saloon, mounted John Murphy's saddle pony at the hitching rack and loped out of Fort Grant on the Outlaw Trail. The pony was returned to Fort Grant a week later, led in by one of Murphy's friends, who informed him that the Kid didn't care to be labeled a horse thief.

That same year Billy the Kid arrived in Lincoln Town on horseback looking for a job as a cowboy. Even then, as some reports have it, he was a young tough and slick at the gambling tables. He was said to be slender, five-foot-eight-inches tall with light brown hair and cold-steel eyes. Freckles and buckteeth didn't keep him from being described as handsome. He had a cheerful nature and was good at the fandango. He was generous with his money and the girls about town nominated him a favorite. He was considered honest except for occasional cattle rustling, because a man has to make a living.

In January, 1878, Billy went to work for the wealthy young Englishman, John Tunstall, on his ranch on the Rio Feliz a thirty-mile buzzard flight south of Lincoln. Billy took an immediate liking for Tunstall, the first real friend to enter his young life. John Tunstall liked Billy for his winning ways and skill with horse and lariat.

But Tunstall invested sufficient capital in something reckless. He had opened a mercantile business in Lincoln that year before, in competition with the Murphy-Dolan enterprise situated in the "Big House" a short distance up the street—politically powerful, suppliers of beef on contract to the military at Fort Stanton and the Mescalero Apache Indians. Wagon trains down from Las Vegas, Santa Fe, and eastward from Socorro on the Rio Grande hauled merchandise of every description to stock the Murphy-Dolan shelves, bins and barrels. Lawrence G. Murphy was not only wealthy with cash but unhealthy in influence. His prosperity was backed by Thomas B. Catron, president of the First National Bank of Santa Fe and leader of the notorious "Santa Fe Ring," a clique of Republican lawyers who controlled by shady methods the politics of New Mexico.

Tunstall had taken a partner, Alexander McSween, a Scots-Canadian native of Prince Edward Island, later a Kansas attorney. His presence in Lincoln came about when he was hired in 1876 by the estate administrators of the deceased Colonel Emil Fritz to collect on a $10,000 insurance policy, the Fritz family of Spring Ranch being associates of John Riley of the Murphy-Dolan company.

At the time of the McSween-Tunstall partnership the Lincoln County Bank was opened in their store, with John Chisum as president. McSween was vice-president and Tunstall treasurer. This spelled competition for Murphy and Catron when huge beef contracts were granted Tunstall, via Chisum. Then the feud sparked, kindled and broke into open hell fire. Factions were formed by sympathizers of Murphy-Dolan versus friends of Tunstall-McSween. Christmas of 1877 found the sun over Lincoln county shining as bright as ever, but with an air of trouble rustling the settlements, and the ranches, mountains and grasslands. And about a month after that fateful Yuletide, Billy the Kid came onto the scene.

Trouble began in earnest when the Fritz family accused McSween of using the collected insurance money for his own purposes, obtaining a court order. Tunstall, in turn, penned a letter to a newspaper to the effect that Sheriff William Brady had given county tax funds to Murphy and Dolan for paying off their debts.

February 18, 1878, found a posse led by Deputy J. B. Matthews on the trail to Tunstall's ranch on the Feliz, sent by Brady with a warrant to seize some cattle. They met Tunstall on the way, he riding toward Lincoln. Shots felled Tunstall and his horse. And now, with a friend of friends lost forever, Billy the Kid swore to all the county an oath of deadliest vengeance. It was satisfied the following April 1 when Sheriff Brady and Deputy Hindman were ambushed and killed on the street in front of the McSween store.

Open warfare broke out along the street, Murphy agents suspecting everybody, McSween feudists doing likewise. Killing was the order of any day, gunmen firing at random. The culminating battle was fought on the street at the McSween store on July 19, 1878, lasting three days, when McSween was killed and his house burned. Four other men met their deaths in the gunfire. Billy the Kid fired away, and when the smoke cleared he and his followers had ridden out to the latitudes beyond the Capitans, there to enjoy a couple years of cattle rustling and light-hearted sinning. There was talk, however, of incidental killings.

Lawrence Murphy had departed the scene before the shooting began, moved himself to Santa Fe a very sick man and died there in October of 1878. Riley gave up his partnership, left town, so business at the Big House was carried on by Dolan, operating as J. J. Dolan & Co. But only for a short time. He inherited the huge debt left by Murphy and Riley and was forced into bankruptcy.

While Billy the Kid and his bunch ranged free, the killing of Sheriff Brady and his deputy still burned hot in the sentiments of certain people in Lincoln who were firm in their belief that murderers, like horsethieves, should hang for their crimes. The following year, in February of 1879, Billy happened to be in Lincoln and witnessed the shooting of a lawyer. Governor Lew Wallace of New Mexico arranged a meeting, secret from the town folk, on the long porch of the Isaac Ellis house, where he asked the young outlaw if he would testify before a grand jury. Billy agreed after a pact was made. He was to give himself up to a new sheriff and testify to the murder he witnessed, then stand trial for all the charges against himself. If convicted, it was promised, the governor would most certainly have him pardoned. Which, if the guiding light of outlaws and lawmen hadn't behaved in so fickle a manner, the wild and wooly career of Billy Bonney, alias Kid Antrim, would have come to a happy climax. But the case was moved to Mesilla, in Dona Ana County, where Billy had few friends. There he escaped from jail, feeling that the governor had not kept his word.

The year 1880 came along with Billy and his gang getting into trouble, this time for stealing cattle. Several posses took out after them, but the jolly rustlers dodged them all. The boys rode free for the summer months, Billy with "the best pals a feller could have," Charlie Bowdre and Tom O'Folliard, friends who had stuck with him when the gunfire raged hot in old Lincoln Town. But changes in Old Lincoln were taking place, too, and some folk there were "plumb saturated" in the prediction that Billy the Kid's reckless days would be coming to a close pretty darn quick. For a new sheriff had been elected, one out of Texas, tall and honest, with a nimble trigger finger and an eye with a glint the color of steel.

Pat Garrett was first a cowboy and horse wrangler in the Fort Sumner area, and as such had met Billy the Kid on occasion. He was six feet four inches tall in his stocking feet, and in cowboy boots he rightfully earned a nickname given by horseback men, Juan Largo, or "Long John." He was celebrated for his skill, sense and long-suffering in dealing with cattle, and how he had the knack of riding down to good sense any "chisel-headed outlaw horse." And it is common knowledge in the cow country that if a man can deal justice to an outlaw horse he can do the same with outlaws.

So Pat Garrett was duly elected sheriff of Lincoln county, and he took official quarters in the upstairs of the old Murphy-Dolan "Big House" which that same year had become the courthouse of the huge county. Friends of the murdered Sheriff Brady were still "chewing at the bits" for someone to bring to the gallows the small bowlegged freckle-face who had committed the crime. So Sheriff Pat Garrett, with a posse, took out on horseback for the purpose of satisfying their hunger for revenge, and for the good name of the Territory of New Mexico.

Pat Garrett and the posse caught up with the Kid at Fort Sumner, and with his friends loyal to the last days of their own reckless lives. There was a gun fight and a bullet snuffed out the life of Tom O'Folliard. The rest of the gang, including the Kid, managed to escape. Three days later Garrett's men surprised them at Stinking Springs, in the Fort Sumner area, killed Charlie Bowdre and captured the Kid along with the remnant of his followers.

Billy the Kid was jailed in Santa Fe before his removal to Mesilla for standing trial—charged with the murders of Sheriff Brady and his deputy. The jury found him guilty and sentenced him to be hanged in Lincoln on Friday, May 13, 1881. He was taken from Mesilla to the Lincoln jail by Deputy Sheriff Bob Olinger, a man later to play a leading part in the drama.

But Billy the Kid was never born to be hanged. His place of confinement in the Lincoln jail was a small room at the northeast corner upstairs of the courthouse, held seated in a chair except for periods of exercise and trips to the privy, always with a guard nearby. His special guards were Bob Olinger, who had brought him to Lincoln after his sentencing at Mesilla, and J. W. Bell. Both deputies were respected men throughout the county, but some writers of the Billy the Kid saga described Olinger as a sadistic prankster fostering hate for himself by reminding this particular condemned of his forthcoming doom and the nasty feel of the rope.

On the fateful evening of April 28, Billy freed himself of handcuffs while Deputy Bell was away for a few minutes, and while still in leg irons, helped himself to a loaded rifle in Garrett's office. He then waited at the head of the stairway for Bell's return.

Olinger, at the time, was across the street at the Wortley Hotel, feeding himself and some trusty prisoners with a taste of supper. Whatever item he enjoyed from the menu was disturbed by the sound of rifle shot across the street in the courthouse. He threw down his knife and fork and made tracks toward the disturbance.

Two shots had been fired at Bell as he made his way up the stairway—the first missed, and the second struck the deputy broadside of the head. The Kid descended the stairs, in leg irons, invested himself of Bell's cartridge belt and holstered six-shooter, and made his way back to the second floor, to the open window overlooking the street in the very room where he had been shackled.

"Hullo, Bob," he greeted the deputy who was hurrying to investigate the commotion. Olinger looked up to see the grinning face of Billy the Kid at the window, then departed life when a bullet from the aimed rifle shattered his head. And it was then that the Kid dragged his leg irons to the balcony and slid down the post, with the entire population witnessing the escape.

Old Man Goss, a county employee then at the door of the courthouse, stood aghast at what he saw until the Kid ordered him to the corral and fetch a saddled horse. By Luck of the Outlaws, the county clerk, then probably in a saloon down the street, had his pony already saddled in the corral. Old Man Goss obligingly brought it forward for the Kid's convenience. The Kid demanded a file for cutting apart the chain holding his leg irons, so Old Man Goss obliged. Then, with the chain severed, Billy the Kid mounted the horse and rode out of Lincoln waving an "Adios" to watching admirers and adversaries alike. A report has it that the lumber waiting to erect the gallows for Billy the Kid was used to make coffins for Bell and Olinger.

April departed the following Sunday, May ran into June, and where in the world was Billy the Kid?

Hoof tracks indicated that on making his escape he had ridden west out of Lincoln, crossed the Bonito and followed Baca Canyon to the bench of the Capitans. He'd probably crossed The Gap and found hospitality among his many friends in the vicinity of the Block Ranch and Las Tablas, obtained a fresh horse and guns after he'd been completely freed of his dangling leg irons. Then, if he had any sense at all, he'd have loped hell-bent south to the sanctuary of Chihuahua, Mexico, never to risk his presence in New Mexico again.

In the early part of July, John Poe, a law officer with the Canadian River Cattle Association, was in White Oaks investigating some beef hides that wore brands of stolen cattle. At the hotel he was approached by a man he had known in Texas, a whiskey-soaked patron of the town's many saloons. He gave Poe to know that if he could trust his confidence he could render some valuable information. Poe agreed, and in a low voice was told that, since the escape, Billy the Kid had been seen in White Oaks on occasion and was then in the Fort Sumner vicinity. He attributed his knowledge to a recent night spent in a storeroom in the Dedrick & West livery stable, there to nurse a bottle of whiskey, and had overheard through the thin partition wall two friends of the Kid discussing the outlaw's whereabouts.

Poe could hardly believe what he heard, but gave the drunk enough coin to buy a quart of Old Tanglefoot, and took off on a fast horse around the Patos Mountains and over the Capitan Gap straight for Lincoln Town. Garrett, like Poe, couldn't believe the drunk's story. The Kid may have been reckless, but not that much a fool. But any tip was worth following, so Garrett and Poe took off for Roswell, where resided a deputy named Tip McKinney. McKinney was skeptical, but willing to make the eighty-mile ride to Fort Sumner if there was any possibility of ridding the good earth of such sorry flesh as Billy the Kid.

The three made the distance in two days, the first thirty miles mostly in cover of darkness, and the fifty-four thereafter in open daylight. They skirted Fort Sumner to arrive at the Sunnyside ranch of Milnor Rudolph, a member of the prominent Las Vegas family. Nine miles south lay the small settlement where the ranch house of Pete Maxwell was located. When asked if he knew of the Kid's whereabouts Rudolph denied he had heard anything—but he denied it so nervously, stuttering as though his life was in jeopardy, that the lawmen were certain he was lying.

If the Kid was there, everyone knew it, and everyone out of respect for the outlaw or out of fear of reprisal would keep what they knew secret. He had friends, Saval Gutierrez and his wife Celsa, whose house was but a short distance from Maxwell's. The Kid could be hiding out there. But, again, would he try anything as risky as that?

Before dark set in John Poe rode into the village. He was not known to the two or three hundred inhabitants, but was eyed with suspicion nevertheless. They kept an untrusting silence, and the very air suggested that the Kid was there and about. Poe returned to join Garrett and McKinney at Rudolph's ranch.

When the clear moonlit night overtook Fort Sumner the three lawmen rode into the settlement. They would try questioning Pete Maxwell, but were certain he would remain as silent as the others. They corraled their horses and walked the short distance to the house, the dark silence covering them.

Garrett found Maxwell's bedroom that opened onto a porch. He entered stealthily while Poe and McKinney hunkered down against the outside wall. He talked in almost a whisper with Maxwell, who, of course, claimed he knew nothing of the Kid's whereabouts.

But luck runs out on the best of outlaws in time, and this night of July 14, 1881, was the hour reserved by fate for special dealing with Billy the Kid. For several days past the Kid had been staying at a sheep camp a short distance from the town; and knowing the ways of lawmen of the time, the herder kept urging the Kid to mount his horse and "*Vaya se!*"—to ride hard and find sanctuary in Mexico. El Paso, the nearest point on the border, lay two hundred thirty miles southwestward, and one small horse and rider could make the distance undetected through so vast and empty a country. Besides, he'd find many friends along the way.

"*Mañana, por seguro,*" the herder was promised. Tomorrow, for sure.

The Kid had promised the same to Celsa Gutierrez, and here he was, this night, stealthily making his way to her house on foot.

He was hungry, he informed her on arrival. Again she implored him to ride for Mexico if he had any love for her, for Saval, or for his own life.

"*Mañana,*" he assured her. "But now I am hungry."

Celsa told him that Pete Maxwell had butchered a yearling that day, and, giving him a butcher knife, suggested he go to the porch by Pete's bedroom and cut himself a steak. The Kid had removed his boots, easing his feet after the long walk from the sheep camp. So with knife in hand and barefooted, never without his holstered revolver, he made his way through the darkness to the hanging beef.

But the steak was not to be cut by Billy or fried by Celsa. The Kid spotted Poe and McKinney squatting against the wall, out of the moonlight half-hidden in darkness.

"*Quién es?*" the Kid said, alarmed and wondering. "Who is it?"

The lawmen kept silent, not moving a muscle.

"*Quién es?*" he said for a second time.

No reply, so he moved into Maxwell's bedroom.

"Pete," he said to Maxwell in Spanish. "Who are those men?" He stood at the open door framed in moonlight.

Garrett squatted himself behind Maxwell's bed, his head close to the pillow in order to talk in a whisper as he questioned the rancher under the blanket.

Then, in a flash, no longer than three seconds of time, two shots were fired in quick succession. Then Billy the Kid staggered into the bedroom and fell to the floor. The first shot from Garrett's gun pierced the ribs and stopped in the heart. And the most celebrated outlaw in the history of the West *died without his boots on.*

I like to remember Lincoln Town as it was fifty years after Billy the Kid and the Lincoln County War put the quiet little village into turmoil, when I would ride horseback through it in the late 1920s and early 30s, on my way to the Hondo and back, down from north of the Gap of the Capitans where my home was at the time. The very air of the place was scented with peace, the wide lane dusty and unpaved, the great cottonwoods, box elders and tall poplars green from feeding on the underground reservoir of the Bonito.

I remember the historic courthouse so aged and mellowed, then a school or community center or some sort of meeting place, after the county seat had been moved to Carrizozo in 1913. And the houses were of the town's own special architecture bright with trumpet vine or weeping willow, clean with the smoke of juniper or piñon, the sweetest on earth, drifting from the chimneys.

I remember the lacerated forearm that Doc Woods bandaged for me one day after I had ripped it on barbwire at a ranch on the Hondo, and the simple purchases I made while traveling through at the old Tunstall-McSween store, then operated by John Penfield and his wonderful family, with my saddle pony and bed horse hitched at the long gallery while I conducted the business of myself versus a can of tomatoes or green chili, a box of saltines, perhaps, for a supper before tackling the last lap on my trip to home beyond the Capitan Gap. A wave of "Howdy" to Fred Pfingsten, the Southern Pacific's own great "water man," on whom irrigation of the Bonito Valley depended as well as the locomotives down at the rail yards in Carrizozo—maintainer of White Mountain water, the sweetest, softest imaginable.

Lincoln Town, so blessed with serenity, so far from the trials and bogus blessings and noise and commotion of an unrelated world!

But now, it is a full hundred years since Pat Garrett's bullet put Billy the Kid to eternal rest and the Lincoln County War ended.

The restored Old Lincoln Courthouse is a museum, state-owned and operated, throbbing daily with tourist patronage; the Tunstall-McSween battle ground is a state monument; the Sam Wortley Hotel has been rebuilt and is serving guests again. Homes of the pioneers have been stabilized for exhibition. The Torreon, circular rock-walled watch tower of 1855, seems ready for a Spanish sentinel to man its roof. Roman and Theodora Maes's La Paloma Museum, directly across from the courthouse, houses probably the finest collection of frontier exhibit pieces in America. And the Pageant grounds where the shots and hard-riding of Billy the Kid presents entertainment for thousands annually in the first week of August.

Because Billy the Kid met his death in Fort Sumner, and is buried there beside his old pals Tom O'Folliard and Charlie Bowdre, that town too must have its share of high jinks commercializing on the pint-sized badman. Tribute of thousands at the grave, even the occasional theft of the tombstone by some trophy-hungry tourist. These are events featured any time of the year.

But the big June spectacle tops the homage and "devotion to the memory" dramatized in Lincoln, or at least equals it. There are cutting horse contests and a golf tournament, a reenactment of a bank robbery, a Western film festival, a Western beauty contest, a melodrama, an arts and crafts show, kids' dog show, a church camp meeting, gunfighters exhibition, pony express race from Stinking Springs to the old fort, Raisin' a Ruckus country music concert, antique car show, rodeo, re-enactment of the death of Billy the Kid. And to top it all the grandest spectacle,

The Tombstone Race!

This event features a fifty-yard run over four- and five-foot barriers, contestants carrying an eighty-pound stone. The winner receives a $1000 prize and a hundred-pound replica of the sanctified tombstone.

Fiddlers' contests, dances, and
more, much more!

All in commemoration of a pistol shot that laid to death a bare-footed ruffian with a butcher knife in hand, on the same Fort Sumner earth on the night of July 14, 1881. And may the gods of ballyhoo smile with satisfaction on the noise and frolic of it all.

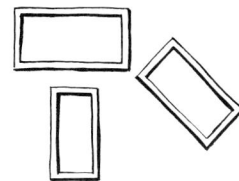

Five
The Block Ranch

Back some fifty-five years ago, when Cowboy Riding Country was in its prime, no one in the area of the Block Ranch knew the actual extent of its range. Taylor the foreman knew, so did the Spencers who owned it. The cowboys who rode for the outfit were familiar with every wide flat and arroyo, saw how the cattle of the triple brand grazed high into the timber of the Capitans and far out on the big and rolling plains to the north, northwest and northeast of headquarters. It was, at the time, one of the best examples of the pure uncontaminated-by-progress cattle breeding establishments in New Mexico.

"How many sections you reckon they've got in the Block pastures?" was a question that went around the countryside, mostly among the nesters and the folk of the smaller ranches, because anything concerning a company the size of the El Capitan Livestock firm was nobody's business. It could have comprised all together three hundred square miles of territory, or even four hundred, every square mile termed a section. I made a guess of two hundred, which was close, when, in casual conversation, the extent of the Block empire was revealed to me in simple, idle talk relative to horses. If in a quandary, or should any puzzle afflict the mind, give the matter to horses and the truth will come out.

It is easy enough to determine the extent of a farm, even a large farm in some rain-blessed, green-fresh section of America where 450 acres of field and pasture comprise the making of a family's living, even a large family—where even 200 acres would be sufficient a slice of the land. Within a farm's boundaries the names and number of the cows and horses, the ways of swine and poultry, have so familiar a place that their movement any hour of the day and night could be kept on record in the farmer's mind.

But what about the *ranches*, so distinct from the *farms* of the Southwest?

In Cowboy Riding Country no land-holding, owned, leased or rented—maintained for a man's living and comprising less than four sections (2,560 acres), could be termed a ranch. It was rated merely a place. Four square miles of grass in range country, where cattle live solely on grass, water, and block-salt, would support perhaps sixty mother cows, and the sale of calves from sixty cows offers scant living for any family, even if such a small herd, as was usual, calved a crop of 90 percent. (On the very large ranches the calf crop would run to 50 percent, often less.)

In 1926 the huge Diamond A ranch of the Bloom Land & Cattle Company, west of Roswell, branded 7,000 calves, an indication that the range carried 15,000 mother cows. And the calf crop was less than 50 percent. The size of the Diamond A land area was pretty well known. It extended in a southeasterly direction from the Circle Diamond on the Hondo River, just downstream from Picacho, to Walnut, a camp west of Artesia by a few miles. Its length was fifty miles, twelve miles at its widest, one mile at the narrow northwest tip. The land area contained 450 sections, that many square miles, or 288,000 acres. There were three main camps: the Diamond A headquarters on the Hondo about fifteen miles west of Roswell, the Circle Diamond near Picacho; and *Five*, the camp comprising a large bunkhouse for cowboys and an extensive corral system for working stock, so was home for the wagon boss, or range boss, manager of all cattle operations. When the chuck-wagon went out on a roundup, or on a trail drive, it left from Five. Jim Decker, Elv Chandler, Gus Chandler, and Montie Flack were the best known of the Diamond A wagon bosses, the most expert cowboys ever to ride for wages in New Mexico, and who will live in legend for their riding, roping and "horse sense" abilities.

About four hundred wild horses grazed the pastures in the 1920s, mostly "mockeys" (mares), and "condemns," ponies too much given to bucking, cold jawing or assorted nasty habits to be useful for "cow work." The Bloom Cattle Company branded its horses with a Circle Diamond on the left shoulder ◈ in contrast with the familiar Diamond A ⩔ on the left ribs on the cattle. The condemned geldings that were noted for a bucking or cowboy-killing talent were given special affectionate names, each with the prefix *sweet*. There was *Sweet Roses* out there idling his life away, and *Sweet Baby*, and a dozen other saccharine devils equally notorious. *Sweet Milk*, the captain of them all, was probably the arch-murderer in the equine community, each pound of him dedicated to crippling cowboys, to exhibit his hate for human society by ways too brutal for refreshing to memory.

Yet Sweet Milk was sometimes roped and hog-tied and saddled while helpless on the ground. Some reckless soul was invited to try at converting the famed outlaw into a mess of buttermilk. No cowboy, as far as it was known, could stay astraddle that horse. Will James, the famous cowboy-author-artist of Montana, has written that "there never was a horse that couldn't be rode." But in spite of the maxim from one who knew, nobody ever rode Sweet Milk for more than half-a-minute, and that truth was gospel-pure throughout New Mexico's Cowboy Riding Country!

Horses were so plentiful in the 1920s that good young geldings were readily selected for breaking into sensible cowponies equipped with the required action. And they were *ponies*, weighing between eight hundred and a thousand pounds. They comprised all colors—browns and blacks, sorrels and duns, strawberry roans and grullas (pronounced *grewyas*), bays and chestnuts, paints, greys; bald-faced and flax-maned, zebra duns, palominos, and duns wearing the Spanish Cross—a black line that extended down the back from the ears to the tail, then down the withers to form the sacred symbol. Broken to work, their sale price ranged from ten to twenty dollars.

Few cowboys rode mares, for the gelding was the ideal companion for work on the range. But their riders, even though rough-natured and uncomely to look upon, were at heart sentimental lily blossoms. They were lonely men who had girls on their minds whenever thoughts weren't concerned with horses. So their mounts were given feminine names regardless of the sex. I remember Clara among the Circle Diamond cowponies, and Beatrice, Rachel and Alice—all thoroughly gelded males. And a score others so daintily tagged by bowlegged, leather-seated, unshaven bachelors, the names honoring old girl friends and relatives and certain professionals in the art of tenderness resident in whorehouses all over eastern New Mexico and west Texas.

With fifteen thousand cows on Diamond A grass back in 1926–27, their presence on a cramped 450 sections hinted that the pastures were severely overgrazed. But in truth the huge herd was there only temporarily. A drought had overtaken the company holdings in South Dakota where the forage was short. In consequence, heavy shipments of northern stock arrived in New Mexico to relieve the situation. Lincoln and Chaves counties offered a good stand of range grass at that time. When South Dakota was finally blessed with rain the pastures were revived and the northern surplus returned home.

Both the Diamond A and Circle Diamond brands ranged far and wide over the West, for the Bloom Cattle Company's interests were not confined solely to New Mexico. Another New Mexico ranch was located near Wagon Mound, along with operations in Colorado, and extensive leases on the Rosebud Indian Reservation in South Dakota. We heard, too, that a Circle Diamond horse ranch operated in Saskatchewan.

As much of the property followed the Hondo River and level meadowlike land lay adjacent. Fields had been laid out in the vicinity of the Headquarters ranch, as well as at the Circle Diamond near Picacho. About four hundred acres were cultivated and irrigated, the soil so provident that bumper crops of alfalfa and corn were harvested. The crops were used for home livestock fodder only, none for sale to the outside. Sixty hogs were fattened and slaughtered every fall for supplying the camps, the outer ranches and headquarters with pork, ham, lard, bacon and sausage. About forty cowboys and field hands were employed at the various camps and ranches. Ed Bloom, a member of the owner-family, managed the Headquarters. His own personal cattle ranch, the Two-Link-Bar, was located a short distance down river. Sam Burgner, who branded his own stock VXA, was in charge of the Circle Diamond; Jess Vines looked after things at the Wagon Mound ranch, Jim Decker was out at Five, Sam Butler raised Rafter S mules at Crow Flat. There were cowboys camps at Cherry valley and other remote pastures. Charlie Corn managed the company's extensive sheep breeding department at Walnut. Captain Burton C. Mossman not only ran his Turkey Track cattle ranch east of the Pecos at Buffalo Valley, but as general manager of the Bloom Cattle Company maintained an office on the second floor of the First National Bank building in Roswell, where a beautiful lady dear to us all, his secretary, Mrs. Kelly, made out our thirty-five and forty dollar monthly pay checks. And at the Headquarters Ranch old Lee Crane, a native of Missouri and proud of it, kept the company Model T truck in prime condition for hauling ranch supplies from Roswell to sundry camps and firesides all over the big and lonesome Diamond A territory.

Farming operations, a sheep-raising section, and a truck for hauling in the necessities.

So there in the three elements named, the Diamond A of Chaves county differed severely from the El Capitan Livestock Company's Block Ranch in Lincoln county. Interests of the former were wide and varied, but the latter was cattle-cowboy-pure.

On its fifty-mile downward and southeastward course the Diamond A range spread from the Picacho foothills over the flats and baldies, unrelieved of the monotonous plains landscape. Until the green Pecos Valley came into view, a valley which the Walnut pasture didn't quite reach. There only the sunrise and sunset spectaculars offered color to contrast with the intense yellow midday glow.

The Blocks, on the other hand, had the forty-mile stretch of the Capitan mountains for a south view, the timber beginning to thicken only three-and-a-half miles from the ranchhouse door, a panorama of the majestic culminating peak over ten thousand feet above sea level. The ranchhouse itself was at six thousand feet on Cottonwood Canyon. To the north, west and east the cattle fed on a rolling grama grass prairie. The north side of the Capitans was without foothills, the canyons falling gently from timber to plains.

The Block ranch had a history as dramatic as any in the West, although the headquarters house showed an architectural style equally as commonplace as a white painted frame family dwelling along an elm-shaded street in Connecticut. And white frame it was, two storey with a porch at the front door that appeared to be stuck on with glue. Nothing long and rambling as the Chisum Big House at South Spring, or the low "shotgun" type rock structures on the Diamond A at Headquarters. But it was chuck-full with all the hard-riding, six-shooting drama of the nineteenth-century West. The house where the Block cowboys resided would have made a dull setting for a Hollywood movie production.

The Big Corral, a mile or so to the northeast where the cattle were worked, was something of a different nature. There on days when it served its purpose the dust stirred up by bovine and equine hoofs rose to make haze of the clean high altitude air, when cowboy and cowpony performed their joint exercise of physical skill, when the intricate tactics were lodged in each other's brain. Hark to the din of shouting and whistling as the corraled cattle milled in their excitement. The branding fires crackled with oak and juniper flame. Hurled around was the reek of burning hair as the hot irons were applied. All to a symphony of nickering horses and coarse laughs of cowboys whose wise-cracks tried to brighten the day. There were bawls from bovine mothers concerned about their calves, and the swish of the *heeler's* rope as he selected another victim for the *flankers* to flank at the fire. And most pitiful of all was the helpless, piercing outcry of agony brought on by application of branding-iron, castrating knife, vaccinating syringe, and dehorning cutters.

The history of both the Blocks and the Diamond A stretch back to the mid-nineteenth century. The Diamond A range was Chisum country before the 1870s, when the Bloom family of Trinidad, Colorado, and of Altoona, Pennsylvania—people of the venturesome, hard-working, business-keen "Dutch" variety—blocked up an immense spread of grazing land west of the Pecos Valley and south of Roswell.

The headquarters was established fifteen miles west of town. Camps were at Twin Mills, west of Dexter, and Seven Mile Lake north of that settlement. Another was at Walnut, west of Artesia. All southeastern New Mexico was open range country in the early days, the Diamond A responsible for the first *drift fence* (a barbwire barrier on a straight line with no corners or enclosure) strung to keep cattle from grazing into the valley. Roundups were enormous affairs with several ranchers and their chuck wagons involved. Open range west of the Pecos extended into the Sacramento mountains and the Mescalero Apache country, down beyond the Feliz and Peñasco rivers and the Guadalupes. West of it was open range of somebody else's business, plus his troubles. It was the biggest, most open and reckless country in America.

Sometime after the fencing of the range, when the huge ranch was divided into pastures, another large "company outfit" was purchased by the Blooms—the Circle Diamond near Picacho. All cattle were thereafter branded with the company's original mark, and the Circle Diamond given to identify the horse stock. When the Thatcher family of Pueblo, Colorado, was taken into partnership the company's operations were extended into Colorado and South Dakota.

It was told around the Capitans fifty years ago that in the early years of the Block Ranch cattle of the brand grazed from the Rio Pecos to the Rio Grande, an east to west crow-flight distance of 160 miles. If true, the stock would have fed themselves into Chisum territory at the Bosque Grande, just as the "Cattle King's" U branded stock grazed on Block territory. If conflict developed because of the mixing no mention was made, but if so it would have been just one more dramatic, hard-riding, fast-shooting episode in the long never-quiet saga of the frontier company.

George Curry, the last of the territorial governors, got his first job in New Mexico as handyman on the ranch in 1879. It was a touchy year for Lincoln County. Billy the Kid and his gang had ambushed Sheriff Brady and Deputy Hindman in Lincoln Town the year before, and the killing sent him off on the dodge until he showed up for the Three Day Battle at McSween's store three months later. It was the last violent act of the feud, which again sent the Kid into hiding—off somewhere north of the Capitans with occasional ventures into Fort Sumner and White Oaks. In 1879 a group of prospectors found gold along White Oaks Draw and the bonanza town sprouted from the roots.

Governor Curry told of his one and only meeting with Billy the Kid, and it happened on the Block Ranch. During the summer of 1880, with the Kid and his gang on the loose, the cattlemen of Lincoln county, who included John Chisum as well as the Block men, were more than fed up with the rustling of stock that had plagued the ranges since the end of the feud, and the lawmen seemed to be doing nothing to help the situation. Outlaws and other leeches upon honest business were profiting for their misdemeanors.

George Kimbrell, the incumbent sheriff, was campaigning full force as election day of 1880 drew close. He had been a sympathizer of the Tunstall-McSween faction in the recent "war," and while in office seemed to do nothing about running down and bringing outlaws to justice. He was unpopular with the stockmen but politically powerful otherwise. Now he was running for reelection against a tall Texan recently come to Fort Sumner, who cowboyed on a ranch in the vicinity. This man, Kimbrell's opponent, had a reputation for being utterly fearless, honest and likable, intelligent, healthy and strong, and had the best aim with rifle or six-shooter of any marksman come out of Texas. And he was dedicated, if elected, to bring to the gallows Billy the Kid or any other outlaw besmirching the decency of the county. He was the cattlemen's candidate. But could he win against so powerful an opponent as Kimbrell? His name, of course, was Pat Garrett.

On the Monday night before the election, Curry was left alone with the ranch headquarters. Andy Richardson had gone to Lincoln Town, there to meet with Delaney and drum up support for Garrett among the voters. The night was dark, and cold, and lonely, and a single coal-oil lamp brightened the kitchen. Curry had settled down to some after-supper reading when he heard a "Howdy!" sound itself outside the door. It was a cowboy with a probable request to "stay all night," a frequent occurrence in the ranch country.

Chuck line riders were always welcome, for winter nights could get painfully monotonous. A stranger never failed to brighten things with conversation topics of the outside world. Curry helped the guest put his horse in the corral, throw out some fodder. Returning to the house he set to preparing a fine supper of typical bachelor-cooked cow country fare.

The Blocks ran sheep at the time and several herders were idling and conversing near the corrals. They all recognized the stranger, but the rule of the land was never to mention a name—and above all, never ask! Who knows, the stranger may be an outlaw "on the dodge."

Curry's guest was talkative during the meal, and his chief concern was the upcoming election. The young rider was definitely pro-Kimbrell. He asked Curry if he could predict the outcome of the balloting and was sure that Kimbrell would not only carry the Las Tablas precinct, which included the Block Ranch, but come out victor in the entire county. Curry told him bluntly that in his young opinion Garrett would be the winner, and by a large majority.

"What makes you think that?" the stranger asked.

"Because Garrett is the man Lincoln county needs. He is brave and can't be bought. And he is the *one* man with the stuff it takes to bring Billy the Kid and his gang to justice."

"Then you think he'll win in Las Tablas?"

"I'm sure of it," Curry replied.

The stranger laughed, which seemed to say, "You wait and see." Then he rose and thanked Curry for the meal. He said he was off to Las Tablas where a pre-election dance was under way. He was out to join in and have some fun. He left Curry on the porch and made his way to the corral. From there he'd saddle up and be on his way. But the herders greeted him as he reached the gate. In turn they shook hands and commenced in loud and excited talk, all in Spanish. Curry, fresh to New Mexico and who knew little Spanish, was sure by the tone that the topic was political, for the names of Kimbrell and Garrett came loud and clear.

Curry, standing on the porch, watched the young rider rein his pony up the road leading to Las Tablas. He waved at Curry and Curry waved back. Then the future Governor of New Mexico stepped off the porch and joined the group that was still loud in argument—ready to inform that Curry's supper guest was Billy the Kid.

The next day, when the ballots were counted, the news came out of Lincoln Town that Garrett had won, Kimbrell defeated. Billy the Kid's doom was sealed. Governor Curry took pleasure in recounting the incident in after years, chuckling as he claimed his first loss in offering a political opinion happened when he was a hand on the Block Ranch. Billy the Kid won on that score, for the Las Tablas precinct went for Kimbrell, almost to every voter.

White Oaks, which mushroomed as a boom town in 1879, was located about twenty miles west of the ranch in a wide gap between the Patos and Jicarilla mountains. As the camp went wild with gold fever a few great names in the early Southwest arrived there to spark their careers into fame. There was Ash Upson, for one, frontier journalist; Emerson Hough, author and novelist; Harvey Fergusson, founder of the literary family. Conrad Hilton barely missed being born in White Oaks, but instead saw first light in San Antonio, sixty miles west on the Rio Grande. And William D. McDonald—first a clerk, then county assessor, then manager and later owner of the Block Ranch, and finally to shine in glory as the first Governor of New Mexico after the territory was made a state in 1912.

Curry, along with a distinguished career in the Philippines, served as the second-to-the-last territorial governor. He was a member of the Sixty-second Congress, there at the signing when President Taft proclaimed New Mexico the forty-seventh State. Thus two great chief executives made their mark by first riding the grama grass flats of the Block Ranch.

Prior to the Lincoln County War a huge ranch was established east and west of the Malpais a few miles downgrade west of White Oaks—the Carrizozo Cattle Company, and its owner was Lawrence G. Murphy, archvillain of the notorious Lincoln County feud. Following Murphy's death in Santa Fe, the ranch (Bar W) was sold to an English company and managed by J. A. Alcock, one of the stockholders. The ranch had previously been acquired by Thomas B. Catron of Santa Fe.

Down from White Oaks an ill McDonald applied for a job, and got one as a clerk at the Bar W. Later, this same McDonald became manager—and later yet bought out the same huge company. So successful a cattleman as W. C. McDonald proved himself to be, that he eventually became owner of the great Block Ranch, which he combined with the Bar W as the El Capitan Land & Cattle Company. By the 1920s the name had been changed to the El Capitan Livestock Company. Jack (N. Howard) Thorp, the famous cowboy author, rhymester of the ballad *Little Joe the Wrangler*, rode for both the Blocks and Bar W for several years. Truman Spencer married McDonald's daughter and the company became a Spencer family affair.

The Blocks didn't scatter its camps as much as the Diamond A, simply because it was a smaller outfit. Bill Nix and his wife Lila lived at Headquarters, although his riding territory was the Corn Pasture far to the northeast, once the old 9H6 ranch of the famous stockman clan. Guy Nix and his wife held down a camp at Arroyo Seco, up against the far east end of the mountains.

The cowboys at Headquarters were a mixed lot with varied dispositions, none physically handsome, but all excellent examples of the cowboy mentality, which is the state of mind and opinion that ranks high if confined to the cowboy world—but low in intellectual worth if expressed anywhere else. But the Block cowboys were of the cowboy world. They were athletic, excellent horsemen but could be unkind in their dealing with horses, or with all animals. Prudish around the womenfolks, they were at times foul-mouthed when out with their own male kind, and contemptuous of anyone genteel possessed of creative and original ideas who might have the temerity to suggest that education other than that pertaining to cows was their "sorry lot." Jack Thorp and Eugene Manlove Rhodes maintained the respect of the cattle world in spite of their literary talent, but only because they possessed more athletic talent at bronc-riding, roping and "knowing cows from A to Z."

But there is a boundary. On one side is the Land of the Ranchman and his bowlegged, drawling (as Gene Rhodes termed him) "Hired Man on Horseback"—the sunny and brighter side of the line. It is a domain fiercely ruled by clannish citizens of both sexes, loaded with contempt for the other "region"—which is the world of the "Jellybeans," the "High Moguls," the "Educated Fools."

But wait, all that was Cowboy Riding Country back in the old Block Ranch days of the 1920s. People and conditions have changed. Today the universities and colleges of New Mexico serve the healthy ideas and good sense and sensitive ambitions come off the grama grass flats and high-baldy pastures. Governors and senators and executives and artists and writers and educators and others of such delicate temperament are being made of the cowboy brains the schools nourish. And the Cowboy mentality, slowly but surely, is passing away. As sure as the Longhorn went, they the most colorful of all cattle. The old-time cowboys with their set ideas—as colorful in thought as in speech and looks—remain only a few. Soon they too will pass away. Maybe to an afterworld of their own, where the branding fires of oak and juniper will burn again, and the herds mill around as the riders and cutting horses go to work.

Fond is my memory of the bunch in the Block bunkhouse, fifty, sixty years ago. There was Mr. Birdwell, the headquarters cook. He worked in his cook room with its cast-iron wood-burning range; and barrel of flour, the 32-pound lidded bucket of lard, the shelves from floor to ceiling stocked with Arbuckle's coffee, cans of sugar and heavy sorghum and molasses; wooden boxes of dried peaches, prunes, and apricots—and raisins. (How everybody loved raisins, in pies and boiled with rice and sugar!) There was a mighty slab of bacon hanging in the "cold room" (a small space beside the house open to the outside air, fly-screened at night and closed in with canvas by day), and maybe a ham or two. And large granite bowls of milk, unpasteurized, undiluted, as thick with cream as it came from the cows in the corral. And eggs, a huge pyramid of eggs.

And of all the ingredients brought in by the freight wagon, Mr. Birdwell applied his culinary art on the hot iron of the cook range. Out of its oven slid pans of white flour baking powder biscuits, and great slabs of corn bread. But never, *never*, loaf bread of any kind, which in the cowboy tongue is called "gunwaddin'." White flour baking powder biscuits is "cowboy bread," while sourdough baked in dutch ovens is reserved for the chuckwagon cook, out on camp, along the trail or on the roundup.

Strict etiquette was maintained in Mr. Birdwell's cook room, and around the chuck table. The diners usually kept themselves to the business at hand—eating—saying little except for "Pass the beans," or "I'll thank you for the milk." Plentiful was the supply, but with hungry men at the oilcloth it all seemed to pass magically away.

A very large dishpan was set in the cook room next to the range. This was handy to receive the used plates, bowls and cups, and the "artillery" (forks, knives and spoons) as each diner removed them from the table as he walked his way out. This custom is, or was, strictly maintained on all the large company ranches of the West. It is the cook's duty to set the table, but an insult to his dignity to pick up a man's dirty food-smeared dishes. At the Blocks there was a twenty-five cent fine for anyone who defied the rule, the proceeds going for a new coal-oil lamp or chair or card table for the bunkhouse.

It was up by the morning star, breakfast before daylight, saddle up and ride out just as the sun appeared over the east horizon. And the day's work continued until after the bright fiery light had dropped into night behind the Carrizo and Patos mountains. There were great names known to the cowboy world who at times occupied the Block bunkhouse. Such as Red Dale of Roswell, probably the most expert "cow sense" man who ever rode for a living. Tom Weldy, the opinionated and flavorful cook, who applied his pothooks to dutch ovens handy to the roundup wagon. Roy Roddy and John Lacey, the most permanent of the "hands." And Ed Downing—first a cowboy but also the official ranch freighter.

I never slept a night in the Block bunkhouse, for all the work I helped with was in camp out on the roundup. I lived at the time in a rented log house and horse pasture not far away, and I made an austere living by trotting my saddle pony and bed horse off to short jobs, those frequently available on either the Blocks, at Merchants' ranch, on pastures up by White Oaks and down on Salt Creek. And for better pay at the sheep ranches south of the Hondo, below Picacho and Tinnie.

Two great firsts of my life happened at the Blocks. One event was sitting in rapture in the bunkhouse one night in 1927 as the first radio program ever to meet my ears, *Sam and Henry* (later Amos and Andy), came squealing and squawking from the battery operated device. Another first occurred when, after a ride on the hottest day of summer, I hitched my pony at the door of Mr. Birdwell's cook room, and entered to receive the most cooling invite of my life. The time must have been in the early 1930s.

"John, do you like ice cold milk?" I heard Mr. Birdwell say.

Ice cold milk? I'd never heard of such a thing!

But there it was, a jug of it in a new ultramodern appliance purchased by the El Capitan Livestock Company and set up in a corner of Mr. Birdwell's domain. It rested on short legs, a white-enameled box about three feet square all around, tightly lidded at the top. At the side was a kerosene burner and a coil of tubing. Inside was what appeared to be a metal ball of about eight inches in diameter, and as cold as the Brooks Range of Alaska on New Year's Day. It was one of the very first refrigerators, operated by a small kerosene flame. Appropriately its brand name was Icy Ball. Never in my life before, or since, sunblasted and sweaty as I was, have I ever tasted a more delicious glass of milk!

The most prominent bachelor-cowboy alive in my memory is Arthur Clark, the *brush hand,* who lived with a dog, his horses and a string of burros at the Dockrey Place, an important camp on the Block Ranch. He rode with the nickname Montana, simply because he was born and raised in the Powder River country near Miles City, Montana, and he had been working for the Blocks for several years.

The brush hand is unique among cowboys, with special skills to tackle cattle gone temporarily wild in the thick timber. His horse had to have the brains of a cutting horse and strength of a pony trained for heavy roping, with the patience of Job's donkey and the gentleness of a draft horse, without a trace of the chisel-headed bronc about him.

Montana's day started before daylight when the morning star was low on the horizon. He'd kindle a fire in the cookstove and boil a pot of coffee. He'd let it brew strong and black while he put on his clothes—a simple task pertaining to trousers, socks, boots, and hat, for his night attire was long-handles and shirt. His hat was the first thing he put on in the morning, remaining in place all day, and the last article he removed at night.

The night horse would be in the corral, anxious to be saddled and ridden out to the horse trap for bringing in the mount of the day. With the mount selected and saddled for the day's work, Montana stirred up a mess of breakfast for himself and his dog.

The burro-string was handy nearby, seven or eight in number. Two or three each had a sturdy chain fastened and coiled around the neck, but were free to walk and graze at will. Burro intelligence gave them to know that when the chains are applied they are marked for a day of toil in the mountains.

The Dockrey Place—its house, corrals and series of small pastures—lay at the edge of the timber where piñon and juniper growth gave way to pine, then further up the slope to spruce, fir and aspen. Up there below the rockslides in the thickest timber, Block cattle were feeding on the lush grass—valuable breeding cows and heifers, steers—and if not brought down would go completely wild. And it was the brushhand's business to get them out.

While the sun was hardly above the horizon the five or six of them, Montana on his pony, the dog at this side, the burros ahead all took the trail. Up Peachtree, Peppin or Copeland canyon they went, leaving Kyle Harrison and Millset springs below, where "choused" cattle would head for when given a yell from the rider and bark of the dog. An easy job of cowboying. That's when the scrub-oak brush and loose rocks crashed under fleeing hoofs of cattle going home.

But sometimes a stubborn *owl head* in the bunch, a feisty critter full of spark, one brash enough to exile himself from the sanctuary, would high-tail it upward and deeper into the forest. That's when, at a command from Montana, the dog snapped into action. He'd bark at the heels of the beast until it stopped, head down, horns on the prod, bawling the peculiar sound of fright cattle give when worried by dogs or kindred animals. And trained to do so, the dog kept him worried and bawling until Montana rode up with his heavy lariat. A deft swing of the loop caught the steer around the neck, and the captured animal battled with all the strength he possessed, fighting the dog as Montana eased his catch toward the nearest tree—cowboy, horse, rope, and dog working in joint precision.

The trick now would be to get the taut rope lowered against the tree trunk, as Montana freed his lariat from the saddle horn, employing the *dar la vuelta* (Spanish for *give a turn*) taking up the slack around the saddle horn as the dog worries the captured steer closer toward the rider and the tree. Then with the nimble step of an equine gymnast the pony at Montana's bridle-rein guidance would step over the taut rope and circle the tree, once around, maybe twice. With rope in hand Montana would dismount to bring up the slack, as the steer, with head lowered, came closer to the tree.

The contest goes on as long as there is rope between steer's head and tree trunk. The bawling of the agonized beast is deafening, echoing down the forest slopes, hitting the rockslides and deep canyons. Finally there would come the task of making a *tie* on the rope, the knot that will *snub* the wearied beast to the tree—while the dog, panting, sits down to rest and Montana mounts his pony to bring on the burros.

All the rambunctiousness the steer possessed has by now been worked out after his fight with horse, dog, and man. A chain-yoked burro is led to the steer, as close as possible, where with some cowboy maneuvering the free end of the chain is thrown and locked around the captive's neck. Now it is the burro's turn to lead the quarry home. With about eight feet of heavy chain, one end snapped loose around the burro's neck, the other likewise around the steer's, Montana frees his lariat—first from burro, then steer—and works it into a coil to fit the tie-string beneath his saddle-horn. He mounts his pony and with trailing dog and remaining burros trots off in search of the wild ones. Some that with only a yell and a bark will stampede for home down the mountainside. Or, perhaps, meet with a stubborn one, a candidate for the rope, tree, dog, chain and burro treatment.

Meanwhile, steer and burro chain-yoked together, start their trip for the Dockrey Place. Maybe the delivery will require a couple days, and again the course of a full week. But the trained burro will get the job done, leisurely grazing as he goes. Job's donkey had the patience of his master, likewise Balaam's, and all the shaggy, long-eared, domesticated asses of Asia, Ireland, and the Mother Lode. Equal for their worth and purpose were the burros of New Mexico. The Dockrey Place contingent was a sterling example of the breed.

So life was tough-going on the Block Ranch in the days when a cowboy earned every dollar of his wages, dried up his hide and broke his bones by sunup to sundown labor, mounted or afoot. Work that was sometimes unnecessarily cruel. His was a sacrifice that only the hardiest, most callous men could survive. Much of the work force was almost to a man uneducated, rough and contemptuous, often dishonest, unkind—but loyal to his own kind and the sweat and toil to which his days were committed.

And probably heading the roster of stern, cruel, inhuman, born-to-be-hated ranch foremen within the boundaries of the American West was Tom Pridemore, a wagonboss of the Blocks, there at the turn of the century. The legends told of this man would fill a volume, cruelties inflicted on man and animal that only the poisoned heart of Count Dracula could engineer. There were legends galore, most without base or reason.

Tom Pridemore, it was told, hated horses and the men who rode them; he was inhospitable to chuck-line riders, charging them for supper and breakfast; he performed the most diabolical practical jokes, not only setting cockleburs in the underside of a cowboy's saddle blanket, but catching rattlesnakes and introducing them live into bunkhouse bedrolls; just two of a thousand ingredients that made Pridemore's nature. There is a very steep hill at Block headquarters rising as a cone from the prairie level, at the foot of which repose two bodies in unmarked graves. It is told that Pridemore amused himself by challenging a cowboy's riding skill. Rider and horse climbed to the summit then descended the steep side at a high lope. Hence the reason for the presence of the two graves. But oldtime cowboys who had actually worked for the martinet explained to me that Pridemore was an expert at getting lazy hands down to work.

If the old-time rangerider had a touch of tenderness about him it was the distaff side of Cowboy Riding Country that was responsible for its power to bless. I remember the Saturday night dances at Pine Lodge, a log-constructed resort for Roswell folk, fifty-five miles west of town in the thickest of Capitan mountain timber. The Lodge was surrounded by pine and spruce that seemed almost as tall as the peaks. Saturday night features were square dancing, fox-trots, waltzes, all to music of the Capitan Mountain Boomers. The huge log-walled hall was bright with kerosene lanterns hung from the rafters, and the sprinkling of cornmeal on the dance floor helped the action of sliding and tapping feet.

The girls up from town or in from the ranches were bright in their festive dresses—correct in the fashion of the late 1920s. Through the open windows came the evergreen perfume of the forest, and out through the same windows trilled the sound of music, came the caller's guiding of the square dance. Outside were the corrals where the cowponies rested and groups of cowboys gathered in lazy conversation, away from the fast motion of the dance. And through all the years of the Pine Lodge dances I attended, never once did I witness a show of drunkenness or rowdy behavior. But beside the dance floor

I'd watch the roughest of men convert temporarily to the delicate nature dormant within them, as they glided their partners around the floor to the quiet strains of *Springtime In The Rockies*, or *The Waltz You Saved For Me*.

And with the *Home Waltz* the dance was finished. Soon after, sunrise brightened the mountain slope, when the summer-green prairie was spread below, to the north, to the east, to the west; in the fresh morning light the grass turned golden in the loveliest hour of the day—setting a stage bordered by horizons, the proud domain of the Block Ranch.

And how mighty in land area was the Blocks?

Lloyd Taylor, the foreman, let me know one morning while we watched Ed Downing, the freighter, take off for Capitan aboard his lumbering four-horse freight wagon, reining for the road across Capitan Pass, to "stay all night" at Mother Julian's Board and Rooming House and load up next day at Titsworth's Store with supplies needed for operating a successful cattle ranch.

And while I watched, I thought of old Lee Crane who drove the Model T truck for the Diamond A, and all the rattling Ford and Chevrolet pickups the smaller ranches had invested in—and I wondered and pondered, not knowing that I was about to be enlightened as to how large a spread was the Block Ranch.

I said to Taylor, "Taylor, when will the Blocks ever buy a truck?"

And Taylor said back to me, "John, do you see that big stretch of prairie out yonder?"

While he spoke he spread his hand and swept an arm, to indicate the grassy kingdom from horizon to horizon, the hugeness of it, the immensity.

"Out there lie two hundred and fifty sections that make up every square mile of this outfit. And right in the middle of each section stands a horse, a good healthy one with plenty of action—doin' nothin' but eat grass, drink water and lick at salt blocks. Two hundred and fifty sections, two hundred and fifty horses! And you ask me, '*When will the Blocks ever buy a truck!*'"

Six
The Paterson Place

I knew nothing of the Paterson family other than that they homesteaded one of the nicest 160-acre government claims on the north side of the Capitan mountains. That they moved away after a time to leave the house and corrals to the packrats and rattlesnakes. And that of a large family they were parents of a daughter named Myrtle and a son Bob. I never met Myrtle, but Bob worked as chuck-wagon cook on the roundup along the Patos Draw in 1929. I liked him, as I did the flavor of the chuck under the bar of his potrack.

They must have been a happy lot, the Paterson family, for the house they abandoned had a feeling of peace about it, moreso than any place I have lived in before or since. It was located just north of Capitan Gap, the rocky pass that divides the West Mountain of the range from the piney bulk that stretches eastward for forty miles toward the rolling prairies. The homestead consisted not only of fenced grama grass pasture but a good set of corrals and sheds adjacent to the dwelling. There was a chicken house—and, blessedly, all construction material other than the rusted "tin" roofs were of expertly cut and adzed pine logs.

The cabin contained one room of about twenty by twenty feet, with a lean-to along the west side to a width of eight feet. The metal pitch-roof sagged beautifully, rustic and rusty. A concrete cistern was handy at the lean-to door, fed with rainwater by a downspout from the roof, healthy with iron and soft as down, for household use brought to the surface by bucket and rope. A tight lid kept the underground concrete tank safe from invaders, such as, as Shakespeare put it, "rats and mice and such small deer." Two windows gave light to the main room, while one brightened the lean-to. It was a happy mountain home for one lone bachelor!

Old Man Charlie Dixon, who ran cattle on the southside of the Capitans, grazed a few head of stuff on the Paterson place, mostly during the summer months when the earth tank scooped in the arroyo to catch a flow of rainwater held its contents. He used the pasture's summer growth of grass to succor the cattle. Old Man Charlie Dixon trailed his stuff back across the Gap when winter set in.

All of which left the cabin vacant and the cistern unused, and the corrals with no purpose at all other than to fall down sick with disrepair. So Old Man Charlie Dixon offered to rent me the place for five dollars a month, or sixty dollars a year—an ideal setting for my chosen way of life. I could graze my three saddle horses, and Old Man Charlie Dixon would sell me enough Blue Andalusian hens and a rooster for restoring life to the chicken house. By agreement I would keep the fences in repair, and rebuild the corrals which, of course, would be to my benefit. So I paid out five dollars for the first month's rent, inspiring my landlord to say, "I hope you and your horses will like your new home." He didn't say anything about cats, which he supplied later along with the chickens.

Throughout the 1920s, the years I knew it best, the surrounding Capitan mountain country was a vast sea of range grass, with islands of cedar breaks. There were red-earth arroyos here and there on the immense flatlands. The towering island rising out of the grama sea was the mountain itself, a tapestry of pine and spruce, aspen and hemlock and balsam, Douglas fir, juniper of fernlike branches, piñon rich with pitch. A sparse supply of arctic wildflowers brightened the peaks above timberline, not too lofty as New Mexico's mountains go, the culmination at a moderate 10,000 feet. The range was dubbed *dry mountains*, with no springs of water along the summit-backbone but many gushing along the sides. In the summer season sheep grazing the high meadows found sufficient watering in the heavy morning dew. Trails down the south side followed canyons that lowered into the Bonito Valley and offered views of Lincoln Town and Capitan. The north view from the summit offered only the endless sweep of the cattle country, nothing but grass and horizon. To the northwest ranged the Carrizo, Vera Cruz, Tucson, Patos and Jicarilla mountains—and dimly grey on the faraway skyline could be seen the Gallina and Manzano chains. At the very east end of the Capitan Mountain the slope dropped to a jungle of rock spires called the Devil's Playground, so named because lightning had a picturesque way of dancing from one God-sculpted monolith to another as the thunder crashed and the storm made merry.

Wildlife, of course, was in profusion, deer, bear, mountain lion, wild turkey and eagles, and an assortment of lesser furred or winged creatures. Apparently they all accepted me for a neighbor. Smokey the Bear—in later times a national symbol used by the Forest Service to promote forest conservation—was a native of the Capitan mountains. A bird in flight against a blue or stormy sky, or one at song on a tree limb, was education for me in the craft of dealing with my fellow humans. The clean independence of them. The self-sufficiency, pleading to be left alone. I admired the packrat for his industry, and cautiously respected the rattlesnake for his desire to coil at my doorstep; not that he had animosity for me, but as mice were his diet he knew the latitude of his larder—for human habitation and little rodents seemingly go together, especially in rural households. And in my *loneness*, never *loneliness*, I learned much from the birds and furry things: a violent distaste for anything resembling a gun, or weapon, or a device to kill. I owned a gun, and sufficient ammunition, but to use only for my own protection. The gun as an article of the hunter was the business of my mountaineer neighbors, not to be interfered with, as they in turn respected my own personal views of hunting.

Legal hunting season came regularly every November when the residents took cover for the duration, admittedly for their own protection. At that time sportsmen from the valley towns and points in west Texas arrived with guns and ammunition and camping gear, all with a license to show, each bent on the slaughter of deer and wild turkey. Their bent was to shoot at anything that moved. So our nonsportsman folk of the mountains attended to home chores for the ten legal days, to hear in disgust the cracking of rifles and shotguns that blasted the serenity of our environment, seldom venturing into the danger zone.

My neighbors were of a special breed of American. They had mountain and high plains characteristics strong in their blood, put there by a term of ancestry that began in America with the first colonists—pioneers of Virginia and Pennsylvania, of the Carolinas and Tennessee and the deep regions of the South. Out of the South came the Anglo-Texans and Oklahomans—from the Ozarks, the Blue Ridge, and the Great Smokies, from the Cross Timbers and the Llano, from the Big Thicket and the Louisiana swamps and bayous—all to help populate rural southeastern New Mexico.

So the hunting season of my immediate neighbors was not of the legal ten days in November, but one of three hundred and fifty-five days duration. It was perhaps unsportsmanlike of them to prefer their own season and dodge the game warden, but they hunted to obtain food for the table, as their forebears had done for generations past in the new fastnesses of America and the old forests of Europe.

The hunters were selective, bringing home to their families only enough meat they could consume—all respecting the rights of other hunters and extremely neighborly with gifts of venison to friends. Crime as we know it today was something we heard about happening only in distant places, foreign troughs of crowds and arrogance such as Chicago and New York. Plainsmen and mountaineers lived by hard work and austerity, although Lincoln county was noted for its history of violence, outlaws and stock thieves, feudists and the ilk. There were in the area a few families suspected of cattle and horse stealing, seemingly proud of the label put upon them.

There were several moonshiners plying their trade in the mountain thickets and isolated arroyos. But the country was so vast and sparsely peopled that offenders of the social code could easily be avoided. "The Roaring Twenties" thundered away at a distance to the east and the west, but we in the shadow of Capitan Peak were happy in the so-called boondocks. At least, we could be absent from our homes for weeks on stretch, never leaving behind us a padlocked door, always without fear of being burglarized.

So it was a happy summer, that of 1927, when I acquired the Paterson Place, on rent from old Man Charlie Dixon, riding into Lincoln County after working for wages on the Diamond A, for Louie Menneke and ranches along Salt Creek in Chaves county. I had an urge to get away from bunkhouses and steady work. And mine was a forward look toward short jobs on cattle and sheep outfits, when available. None to last more than six weeks or better a few days. Such opportunities would open at lambing time in spring, shearing in the early summer, shipping in fall. Roundups on the cattle ranches for branding or autumn trailing to the railroad loading pens. There were fence construction jobs in the sheep hills south of Picacho and Hondo; and, of course, a lot of chuck-line riding just for the hell of it, a means of being sociable.

But joy on the Patterson Place was found in the long stretches of nothing to do but live the "batching" way alone with my cast-iron heater, bed of blankets cushioned on a canvas tarp, flat on the floor, and a rolled saddle blanket for a pillow. With my cats, chickens, and horses. And glorious nights in kerosene lamplight when I would write notes in pencil on ruled pad impressions of the landscape and folk around me, all I could gather of the vast New Mexico wilderness that was my small world. I hoped then, but never dared disclose my ambition to the ranch people, that the notes and impressions would sometime in the future result in a career of writing for publication. Every book, article and short story that in later years by grace of Providence was mine to achieve, I owe to the silent nights I spent within the rough log walls of the Paterson Place. Or riding my ponies up or down the trails, in the mountains or across the flats. And sometimes hunkered down against my lower corralrail, pitching windies with a neighbor horseman who had stopped by to rest his saddle.

The winter season could be brutal on the north side. From November to March temperatures could drop in clear starlit night to zero or below, and clouds drifting over the mountains could herald a two-foot-deep blanket of snow extending hundreds of miles north and east across the flats. The evergreen slope of the Capitans would be heavy in white or glistening with frost. One spring, while at the Paterson Place, I broke ice on the horse trough, the date being June 12. But in spite of the blizzards and sometimes numbing cold, my cabin kept warm and snug.

I cut firewood a short way into the mountains—cedar, juniper, oak, piñon—hauled to my yard by packhorse. Or sometimes a neighbor would reward me with a cord or two in return for milking his cows, feeding his dogs and chickens while he went on a wagon trip to Roswell sixty miles away. The purchase price for firewood then was two dollars a cord.

I kept the main room of my cabin furnished to masculine taste, spicy with a sort of equine odor. My saddle was hung by a short rope from the ceiling, and the walls displayed such sundry necessities as bridles and bits, lariat ropes, spare latigos and billets. A rancher friend gave me a calendar lauding the merits of the Drovers National Bank at the Kansas City Stockyards, featuring a pastoral landscape replete with contented cows. I had a nail apiece to hang my two hats, one for wear on a trip to Roswell or Carrizozo, maybe once a year to El Paso. The other hat for just riding or fooling around.

But my saddle blanket served a double purpose. A fine Navajo, it fit my pony's back when the saddle was cinched and the latigo pulled, but at night it was added to the comfort of my spread-out bedroll on the floor, for when rolled it made an excellent pillow. History informs us that John Chisum every night of his life slept on the floor of his ranch house, as he did out on camp—on soogan blankets sandwiched between a flapped-over canvas tarp. And I learned, too, that Father Eusebio Kino, the Spanish-Barb breeder and

missionary-pioneer of southern Arizona and Sonora, used his saddle blanket for a mattress and a pack saddle for a pillow. If those historic greats could sleep happy that way, why shouldn't I?

Reading was my favorite pastime. I would read in bed with the kerosene lamp on the floor by my pillow. I had a bookshelf nailed to the wall, an orange crate of two compartments, flimsy but sufficient. And I was selective of my reading matter. In one compartment were the two catalogs in season—Sears, Roebuck and Montgomery Ward. And copies of the *Literary Digest* to which I subscribed. *The Saturday Evening Post* was given me by a neighboring rancher after he had them read, as well as *Collier's* and *The American* Magazine. I read and discarded issues that were "just ordinary," but those containing stories by Eugene Manlove Rhodes, Stewart Edward White, and Guy Gilpatrick I kept and read over and over again. The other compartment was home for a dozen or so treasured books—a couple Jack London novels, *The Poems of Robert Burns*, *The Clans, Septs and Regiments of Highland Scotland*, Pat Garrett's *Authentic Life of Billy the Kid*; *Story of My Boyhood and Youth*, by John Muir, Bram Stoker's *Dracula*—and the volume I read continuously, the blessed one I had brought with me to New Mexico, the one I absorbed sentence by sentence, paragraph by paragraph: *Walden*, by Henry David Thoreau. And that last influenced my whole life.

For much of the year my three saddle ponies grazed idly in the pasture. On my trips away from the cabin, with work in mind, I would use them all; one to ride, another as a change to rest the other, and the third to carry my canvas-tarped bed. Whether my destination was the Hondo hills or the flats east of White Oaks, or west of the Carrizo or Patos mountains, the thirty-five or forty dollars in earnings was a tremendous contribution to my wealth. Forty dollars in those blessed days would insure me of a two-month supply of groceries, oats and corn-chops for the horses, chicken-feed, kerosene, even a new shirt and pair of socks.

The lean-to was my kitchen, the whole eight by twenty-foot area of it. A cook's work bench was solid against the wall, with shelves that served as a cabinet for dishes, sugar and salt, baking powder and the like directly above. A crude table of rough lumber stood handy at the door a few feet from the outside cistern—a stand for the water bucket, washpan and soap-bar, while a towel hung by a nail to the wall. Groceries were stored in three home-made, tightly lidded chests, safe from the raids of my friends the packrats.

Bullsnakes, the largest and most fearsome to look upon of all the reptiles of the district, nonvenomous and prized for their ability to help decimate the pesky rodents, often entered my cabin through a hole in the floor I kept open for the pleasure of the cats. But when a rattlesnake coiled at my doorstep in quest of rats and mice, he, or she, was speedily decapitated. I learned much about the habits of snakes while living on the Paterson Place. And of other reptiles, such as horntoads, water dogs, mountain boomers, various species of lizards, because there were hours of peace and solitude available to give thought and ponder, to try and wonder why, and happily come to a conclusion.

For example, one need not study herpetology to correctly learn the sex of a rattlesnake. The male is larger and sluggish, more apt to coil and rattle and look frightful, but ready to act if something warm, such as a leg or hand, should venture in striking distance of his fangs. But for sheer nastiness, the true aggressor, the coiled diamondback raring for a fight, the head of a fighter loaded with venom—the female.

The cabin contained only one piece of furniture when I took it over—a huge, cast iron, thoroughly worn-out kitchen wood-burning range. The grates under the lids were still usable, with a tank for heating water beside the grates yet able to bless my days after years of service. But the oven, try as it might, couldn't generate enough heat to keep food warm, far less bake a pan of biscuits. And as the nearest grocery store was fifteen miles away, and my only transportation a saddle horse and packpony, I was forced to do my baking outside, adjacent to the cistern. There I built a potrack—two iron pipes set in the ground to support a similar cross piece over a fire that was nested in a half-circle of rocks, the familiar chuckwagon cook's method for preparing cowboy dinners, the baking utensil being a cast-iron dutch oven. Coffee and bean pots hung over the fire from the bar.

There's something special about food cooked over a campfire, as probably anyone knows who has drifted for a time off city streets to picnic in the country. And my camp was as far from city living as home and fireside could get. What's special is the redness of oak coals, and maybe a touch of flavor given by the black soot around the outside of the cast-iron utensils—but most of all by the fresh air, like the steam of boiling coffee from under the lid of the pot hanging on the potrack bar; the yeasty smell of baking sourdough bread, and chili mixed in with the boiling beans. And fried potatoes, be they ever so humble, have a nice fresh air complexion to them when scooped from the skillet.

There was nothing super about the store in Capitan, but the Titsworth Company had everything an outdoor man could want in its grocery, hardware, and dry goods departments. And because of the nature of the rangeland patronage, the most discriminating on earth, nothing artificial was stocked on the shelves. To the cowboy trade the words genuine, undoctored, honest, pure, were the truly important words in the English dictionary, even if the cowboy was a sorry hand at putting words together.

I bought a large and heavy cast-iron heater for the general living and sleeping room. It was of the pot-bellied variety which, when fired with a mixture of oak and piñon, kept the cats and myself warm and snug. The horses would find the log-walled shed outside at their convenience, a roof overhead, and a pile of kaffir corn fodder. The heater was a good one and cost me fifteen dollars. At the current rate it would call for three hundred. Maybe more.

I did my shopping by packhorse in those golden days when a dollar bill was worth its salt at one hundred copper pennies. It was fifteen miles from my fireside by way of Capitan Pass (not the Gap), to the town of Capitan on the Roswell-to-Carrizozo highway. Sometimes I could take the trip to the store there and back from sunrise to sundown. Other times I would put myself and my horses up for the night, to sleep in a mattress-bed for a change, take on some woman-cooked supper and breakfast, and for the sake of vanity get a haircut and shave at Selden Burke's barber shop, a seventy-five cent investment. I bought my meals at Mother Julian's Boarding House—table loaded with country-style food: "eat all you can hold," price of a sitting thirty cents.

In those days a ten-dollar bill had purchase-power extraordinary. I'd hear of a job somewhere around, maybe a roundup in the summer for a calf-branding, at the Blocks or Merchants, or a half-dozen others—short jobs that wouldn't keep me away from home for too long a spell, some a few days duration, others maybe six weeks. There'd be shipping cattle in the fall. Or down on the sheep ranches south of Picacho lambing or shearing or shipping. For Pen and Charlie Fuller, the McKnights, all of blessed memory. Bill Kelsey of Tinnie was contracting the business of building wolf-proof fence for the sheepmen, paying a dollar fifty a day, or forty-five dollars a month and board. Six weeks out on camp that netted me about seventy dollars—a fortune!

Money, or the lack of it, was the least of the cowboy's worries; independence and the dignity of his vocation was all. He was a horseman, which gave him pride, a high perch to look down on the world. With a few exceptions to the rule he was honest; and the environment that was his to live and work in was the cleanest in America. His string of saddle horses was his utmost concern—for without a good mount a good cowboy is no cowboy at all. If he could find a paying job, what the hell! And if he couldn't, what the hell!

Willingly, he'd work for his board and a place to roll out his bedroll—just to satisfy his hunger for the range, to work cattle, to ride, to feel the companionship of his saddle. If, when out of a job, and he owned his own saddle horse, and a bed horse for packing his tarped blankets, he'd ride chuck line from ranch to ranch, to stay all night, then on again until he found someone with something for him to do. For happiness he required little, and asked of his employer the same amount. He was extravagant only in his riding gear, for quality in saddlery and accessories was his chief demand. Being human, he spent a small portion of his earnings in the fleshpots of Roswell, Carrizozo, or El Paso.

There seemed to be an abundance of everything in the world, much of which even the humblest could enjoy. Whenever I made my packhorse trips into Capitan for supplies, I'd ride home with the *alforjas* (packbags) bursting. Bacon cost twenty cents a pound, which I got in twenty-pound slabs. Ham twenty-five cents a pound—$3.75 for a fifteen-pound beauty. Potatoes one dollar a hundred. Canned milk six cents per. Coffee fourteen cents a pound. The price of bread-makings—flour, baking powder, salt, baking soda and yeast for sourdough and lard—wouldn't exhaust a five-dollar bill for a three month's run. A twenty-five pound box (wooden) of dried prunes—$2.50. The same weight in dried peaches, apricots, apples—$3.00. Gallon cans of molasses, sorghum, or pancake syrups went at about sixty cents, and they almost gave away sugar.

And as for clothing, shoes cost $3.00 for the best. Shirts ninety-eight cents, riding pants $1.50. A heavy-weight, sheepskin-lined work coat, the best for meeting a January blizzard on horseback, $7.75. If I should ever have cared to look like a "dude," which I never did, a three-piece men's worsted suit would cost me about $14. But I never had the desire for a "jellybean" hat or a citified suit, or wear a necktie in all my long and youthful years in the cowboy world.

All I really needed in life was there about me, the essentials readily available at Titsworth's store in Capitan. Mail came to my mailbox on Mondays, Wednesdays, and Fridays in the rattly Chevrolet driven by Bob Hale, the carrier. The satanically rough dirt road stretched from Capitan to Spindle, the latter place so small it never got on the map. Twice a year the Sears, Roebuck and Montgomery Ward catalogs came to us over the Spindle Route, gala days when the world's finest literature was ours to feast on.

The Block Ranch sent its freight wagon to Capitan about twice a week, the huge four-horse vehicle driven by Ed Downing—a Block hand who also with his brother John had a fair-sized ranch of his own on the Gallo, north of the Capitans. Ed would make the outboard trip in a day, stay at Mother Julian's overnight, then load up with ranch necessities the following day. I would hook a ride with Ed Downing at times when I needed things I couldn't convey on my packhorse, such as a five-gallon can of kerosene and a sack or two of oats and corn-chops for my horses.

Life there and then was of rustic simplicity, and I a champion of Thoreau's philosophy—"a man's wealth is measured by the number of things he can do without." Blessedly, there was no television, no telephone, no bank account, no credit cards or credit—period. No health or life insurance premiums, no thoughts in those youthful days of sickness or death.

Townfolk could buy butter out of tubs in wedges at twenty cents a pound—which was not for me in my unrefrigerated isolation, where lard had to suffice. No cellophane-wrapped products of the faraway world. Very few automobiles anywhere in the vicinity, even though a brand-new Ford or Chevrolet could be bought for $650. And, for a man of my abounding wealth, no income tax.

A few families along the mountain base enjoyed battery-operated radios. Programs were corny, as corn was popular at that day and age. Amos and Andy sounded off from the tubes as Sam and Henry, and there was Herman and Louie. But most conspicuous after supper was a program from Shreveport, Louisiana, sponsored by the W. K. Henderson Iron Works and Supply Co., with W. K. himself at the microphone.

"Hullo, world, doggone it!" was his self-introduction to the radio audience.

Endlessly he talked of his products and rendered his political views. A zealous pro-Al Smith, anti-Hoover Democrat, he lambasted the Republicans from his "asbestos-lined studio." For music without change or variety he stimulated us with such symphonic selections as *Golden Slippers*, *Hand Me Down My Walking Cane*, and *The Cuckoo Waltz*.

Samuel Johnson wrote that "frugality is the parent of liberty"—and I in those rawhide years had no choice but to be frugal and enjoy the fruits of liberty. With so little of my own, mine the wealth of the clean open land that was my home, all within reach in my cabin or after a short horseback ride. Folk who drove cars got their gasoline at fifteen cents a gallon, and heaven knows what a pittance it took to purchase a quart of oil.

Alone, with two or three miles between myself and the nearest neighbor, I can't recall suffering through a lonely day. And the days were so full that sound sleep protected me from lonely nights. I would ride nearly every day, to keep the horses in shape, although I made a rule never to use a pony for pleasure—but for work and transportation only. Yet it was a pleasure to ride over the flats or in the mountains at an easy gait, in the undisturbed quiet of it all, thinking and planning and composing stories in my mind. The mountains were conveniently there for a subject of meditation—the pines, spruce, the rockslides and abrupt escarpments, the gentle ferns in the damp and shady deeper forest, the native strawberries and raspberries, the wild flowers that had their own place and season, with names as sweet as their stems and petals. Would the Indian Paint Brush make a pastel in words as aptly as on an artist's palette? And the Douglas fir, straight and proud, which lifted its head from the highest earth to the clouds of heaven? In later years, as a writer, I was given the affirmative.

Summit Trail switch-backed up to the highest levels of the mountains from its base at the Divide of the Gap. There, legend has it, Billy the Kid hung a six-shooter on the limb of a tree after making his escape from the Lincoln jail. I think every cowboy in Lincoln County dismounted from his horse when riding across the Gap to search for the relic, hoping to discover a rusty piece of metal under one of the trees.

My pony and I loved to take the Summit Trail. It brought us to a world three thousand feet above the level of our cabin and corrals, fresh in the thin air, meadows more than knee-high in grass surrounded by majestic stands of Douglas fir and slopes blanketed with aspen. Once on the summit the trail quit its switchback to continue eastward along the backbone, to terminate at the 10,000-foot crest of Capitan Peak. And we were not the first to enjoy the solitude, the heavenly quiet that knows no comparison.

Had the hoofs of Billy the Kid's horse ever pounded the Summit Trail? Had Sheriff Pat Garrett found the same consolation there as I had fifty years after his time? And had its sublime peace, not so long before my own, nourished the creative mind of the master storyteller, Eugene Manlove Rhodes? Or swell the pride of Captain Saturnino Baca, of Lincoln Town, for whom the Capitan mountains were named?

I rated myself, then, among the thousands upon thousands of mountain dwellers who count the trees as friends. Among them all there a half-dozen or more limbed and needled individuals I especially admired. So I gave them names. For example, a spruce on the Gap Trail I called Mr. Muir, to honor the Father of Yosemite, a man of my own blood and tongue. And an oak close beside my cabin grew by the name of Henry David. For indeed, couldn't

Thoreau have had a similar friend, though his far less scrubbier at his home by Walden Pond? And D. D. a mighty fir at the highest altitude I named for David Douglas. But the most named of all were aspen whose white bark begged for graffiti. Strong bowlegged men carved their names to be there for the life of the trees, some in a moment of tenderness honored wives and sweethearts—and one, I especially remember, bade farewell to the heavenly scene, his words, *Adios. Sierra Capitana.*

Long before my time a solitary miner named Noble filed a claim high on the side of the West Mountain, reached by a trail leading off The Gap. There was nothing special about Noble's abandoned shrine to the goddess named Lady Luck, the dream from which all prospectors' hopes for fortune spring, nothing special about the caved-in mine shaft and all the rusty metal scraps that lay about. The rotted logs were piled on the rock foundation that once was his cabin, the vanished interior that under the rafters sheltered a man's ambition.

But something naturally beautiful remained. There, with roots nourished by the iron of the wreck, was the most beautiful, shapely and verdant balsam I had ever met in my life before or since.

The fragrance off the frondlike branches was the most satisfying treat for my nostrils, shared only with the deer, the bobcat, the bear, the myriad variety of winged loveliness—by the graceful movement of the mountain lion. For the scent of the balsam is God's gift to the freshness of the forest. The tree was too beautiful to be male.

So I named her Diana, Roman goddess of the Moon, who loved and protected all animals, whose beauty she gave to the forests of the world.

Seven
A Friendship with Casimiro

They called him Casimiro, but that was far from the name he was born to. He was a mystery man to all but his closest friends, and those who knew anything about him were very few. He lived in or near the village of Arabela at the extreme east end of the Capitan Mountains, a sort of ward of the Pacheco family, sheep barons if any deserved the distinction.

Casimiro was a Yaqui Indian come north from Sonora. People who knew anything about him say that his Yaqui name was Casemide Biyesca. This sounded a little foreign to the Spanish-speaking *paisanos* of the Lincoln County settlements, so they changed it to suit their tongues, to a more familiar Casimiro Bosca.

I used to wonder how Casimiro ever got to Lincoln County from way down in Sonora. Did he come with his parents, or did he in later youth ride up here on horseback, following the Rio Bavispe northward from the Sahuaripa and Tonichi? Did he cross the United States border where Arizona and New Mexico come together, say near Cloverdale in the Animas?

In the days when Casimiro was young, a man on horseback could just keep on riding forever and wherever he pleased. Why he chose to live his long life near Arabela, no one knows.

It was no short distance between Arabela and Encinoso, perhaps thirty miles over the roughest dirt road in the state, but a soft and kindly one to a pony's hoofs. Arabela hugged the mountain's extreme east end, with the highest summit (10,000 ft.) lording over the west skyline. Almost from the village yards rose the "Devil's Playground," named for the lightning spectaculars that happened when with an orchestral accompaniment of thunder the fiery bolts struck and danced from one monolith to another in a natural forest of rock spires.

I got to know Casimiro, though ever so briefly, in the summer of 1928 when I was twenty-six. Although a poor judge of an Indian's age I came to a guess that he was in his late eighties or early nineties. Other folks of the region thought so, too. And what a man on horseback!

The pony ride to Encinoso from Casimiro's home was probably his favorite, for we saw him so often. Other times he would ride, folks told, in the other direction—down past Bluewater and Pancho Canyon to Escondido Spring. But wherever he rode he sat his horse as spry and nimble and graceful in the saddle as a man of forty.

He was a strong, heavily built Indian, was Casimiro. Never in a hurry, he rode his pony at a walk or a trot, and the pony was a match for the rider, the kind of mount we all rode at the time, the small but active and terrifically hardy Spanish mustang. The two would take the ruts called a road with the dignity born of their breeds—Yaqui and mustang.

Casimiro rode a stock saddle, of course, one with a rawhide-covered saddle horn. But there was one difference that made this man distinctive, and that was the gear he had looped by a saddle string under each end of the wide saddle swell. His thirty-foot manila lariat rope was at the right side, and on the left a coiled twelve-foot long rawhide plaited stockwhip, buckskin-tipped with a popper, and shot-loaded. When Casimiro found use for the lariat he uncoiled it from the right, but whenever the stockwhip came off its left side string, well, that was the start of a display that made him notorious.

On Casimiro's ride to Encinoso, the great piny wall of the mountains would be westward on his left. To his right stretched the grasses that rolled and swelled northward to the Arroyo Seco, and to the dry lakes appropriately called Cocklebur and Antelope. Cactus Flat and the Arroyo del Macho were south of the great gash in red earth we knew as The Gallo.

Canyons were cut down the green mountains to end on the flats, like Peppin Canyon named for a famous sheriff, and Copeland, named for a pioneer. Las Tablas Creek came down directly south of the Block Lookout Station. There was Peachtree Canyon that watered the hunters' retreat called Fox and Fur Lodge. Then came that deep, deep mystery, a puzzle to our minds as intense as offered by Casimiro, the ruin called *Seven Cabins*.

Seven Cabins reposed in a mountain meadow at almost the 7,000-foot level, seven once-loved domiciles set like wagon spokes in a perfect circle facing a hub. They were a complete ruin of rotted logs that once were sheltering walls and scattered rocks that long ago gave out the warmth from hearths coarsely laid and beautiful to look at. There were broken boards about, all home-sawed, trimmed, adzed and chiseled. These had been ceilings, roof-shingles, shakes or rudely fashioned window frames, and doors that once swung on rawhide hinges. Seven Cabins had been built with love by the hands of pioneers.

Surrounding the meadow were the ever-watchful residents of the forest, the green pine and dark spruce. If only *they* could talk, speak their memories, they alone could unravel the mystery of Seven Cabins, tell us the why and wherefore of the circle and the hub.

And how we labored wondering, offering to each other silly conclusions! A hundred legends were concocted, but only one is worth remembering. According to this theory, a Mormon settled the site. For each of his seven wives he built a cabin, each with a place in the circle, its door facing the hub. At the hub stood a shed, and a corral for livestock, where the man of the family spent his days dressing game, tending a garden, penning the cattle, and doing what pioneers did in the light of the sun.

But when mealtimes came around, and sunset over the western ranges called for supper and rest, this over-spoused "husbandman" made tracks for the *Cabin of the Day*. For as there are seven days in a week, so this settler chose to be fed and cozied by a *Wife of the Night*. Which gave me to think that if he had a sense of artistry, or poetic feeling, strong to match his virility, he could have fashioned a plate to decorate each door—such as Sunday, Monday, Tuesday—or Margaret, Sarah, Beulah, and so forth.

Casimiro could have told us. He alone, ageless as the pine and spruce, could have solved for us the mystery of Seven Cabins. But nobody asked. The folk of the Spanish villages feared him and the Texans were aloof to him and his stock whip and pony.

Then there was the ruin of Las Tablas on the creek by the same name that slowed into a dry grama grass flat near Richardson Canyon. When riding near or over the ruin we used to stop and hunt for any souvenir Las Tablas could offer, just in memory of stopping by, to explore it, dead and silent though it be. We found buttons from uniforms, and coins of the Civil War period, probably lost by troopers from Fort Stanton. Bits of broken crockery and remnants of rusted tools, cartridge shells emptied of bullets, but nothing to indicate the reason for the settlement or how it may have appeared in its long ago life.

Casimiro would have known. He could have explained it all. But he was silent—except for the pad or pound of his pony's hoofs, the crack of his whip, and his chuckling laugh.

I met up with him on only one occasion, one midsummer day. I had ridden the mile from my house to the mailbox at the roadside. It must have been on a Monday, Wednesday or Friday, for only on the three days did Bob Hale drive his mail car from Capitan to Spindle and back, serving the boxes along the way. I let my horse drag his bridle-reins and feast on grass as I sought shade of a piñon, to read a letter I had just then received. I finished and folded the letter, and looked up to see a horseman approaching, his pony kept at an easy walk. It was Casimiro.

Frankly, he *did* look ferocious as was popularly supposed. Of the Piman race, his face was darker than most Indians, very wrinkled with age and sporting a sort of Pancho Villa mustache, as many do in Mexico. He sat his horse as if he were part of the saddle, he was so much at ease. He pulled up beside me and greeted me with the friendliest smile. But the coiled stock whip tied below his saddle swell *did* have a deadly look to it. He dismounted and joined me in the shade of the tree. Our horses nickered to each other as his joined mine to munch on the fresh summer grama.

He said nothing, but chuckled. It was the same laugh that put the fear of hell fire into the people of Richardson, a Spanish village on the Block Ranch, and at Encinoso on the Merchant Ranch. I gave him a friendly invite to set as I sprawled comfortably on the fallen piñon needles. I knew very little Spanish then, having been only five years in New Mexico, but I could make use of "*Buenos días.*" He answered my greeting with a chuckle. He then reached out and patted my shoulder. "*Amigo?*" he inquired.

"*Sí,*" I assured him. He chuckled again, with the kindliest sparkle to his sun-squinted eyes.

Was this the Wild Rider of the Spindle Route, the Whip-Cracking Villain from Los Palos, the source of terror to women in Spanish villages—who upon his approach scurried to gather their playing *niños* and herd them into their houses and shut and bolt the doors? (He would uncoil the whip and spur his mount into a lope. At a full run he would take over the village street, slash at the ground with the rawhide-plaited terror, crack its twelve-foot length in the air, its "popper" letting all and sundry know that Casimiro was in town and was having a world of fun.)

We conversed in sign language due to my ignorance of Spanish.

"Where did I live?" I pointed to my cabin, which showed itself clear on a rise to the south. He nodded that he understood.

"Where did I work?" I swung my arms around indicating "sometimes here, sometimes there," pointing to the Block Ranch, the Merchant Ranch, and across the mountains to sheep pastures south of the Hondo. He smiled. I had made myself clear.

Just then he seemed interested in the letter I held in my hand.

"*Lapiz*," he said, with a finger pointed to my shirt pocket. I handed him a pencil as well as the enveloped letter. I wondered if the Yaquis had a word for "pencil."

He scribbled something with apparent difficulty, and when he handed me back the envelope there in what looked like Islamic script was the blessed word—*Amigo*! Friend! The most precious word in either the Spanish or English language. Even in Yaqui.

Then, to my surprise, he offered the return of my pencil.

Surprised, why of course! I had heard it said a thousand times, a warning that took the countryside any season of the year. "Watch your house, don't let Casimiro inside. Keep him out of your saddle shed, he will steal all you own. He is a thief. When you see him coming, go the other way."

So they not only feared him, but they mistrusted his honesty. They feared the mystery man who cracked the whip, loped through the village to send the *mujeres*, the *niños y niñas*, even the *viejos* scurrying behind closed doors. But look! He had given me my pencil, also the envelope signed with sincerity. He gave me to know he was my friend. Maybe Casimiro would come to my house, that day or any time, I thought to myself. And if he should he could eat dinner or supper with me—like beans and bacon and biscuits or coffee. If he should come for supper, he could stay all night. I hoped he would.

But there is one thing sure—Casimiro wasn't too much of a mystery man to certain Spanish families whose homes circled the Capitan Mountains. They surely knew his history. But if they did they were successful at putting him from their minds. Perhaps the great Spanish sheep barons knew his story, they whose herds ranged the hill country east of the mountains from Picacho north to Cedar Hill—aristocrats like the Fresquezs, the Pachecos—and the families of Don Jose Anaya and the great Don Martín Chavez.

There was talk about, which should have given him at least a little credit among the *paisanos*, a historic fact that he had been a close friend of Billy the Kid some forty-eight years before that day we sat together in the shade of the piñon tree. It was said that in the days of the Lincoln County War, Casimiro had a home and ran livestock of his own, south of Los Palos, the village that became Arabela in the heart of the Pacheco empire.

It is also told that on two occasions the Kid sought Casimiro for help. The first was right after the "Three Day Battle" at the McSween store in Lincoln, of July, 1878, after the outlaw had killed Bob Beckwith and others, when he and his friend Billy Wilson, after a successful escape, came to the Arroyo la Paloso afoot, where they met five Apache Indians returning from an antelope hunt. They tried to bargain with the Indians for their mules, with no success. So the two Billys drew their six-shooters and killed them all. Then they rode the mules to Los Palos and presented Casimiro with a fine gift of antelope meat. In return the Yaqui gave them both a saddled horse and wished them a *Vaya con dios* as they loped off on the long ride to Fort Sumner. To Stinking Springs and their capture. Casimiro was a young man then.

The second helping-hand the Kid received from his trusty friend was after the famous escape from the Lincoln jail, on April 28, 1881, when arriving at Casimiro's *jacal* a few days later he was given a place to hide. Casimiro rode down to Lincoln the next day, to idle around as innocent of outlawry as any law-abiding *ranchero* could be, to enjoy a summer day's drink at the *cantina*, perhaps. But above all listen to the gossip. And the gossip told, as he related it to the outlaw Billy Bonney on his return home, that Sheriff Pat Garrett had sworn on oath before the Lord of Heaven, and to all and sundry on the face of the earth, to find Billy the Kid and kill him on sight—or bring him back to Lincoln to hang.

"Ride south," Casimiro advised him. "Go to Mexico. If you stay in this country Pat Garrett will kill you."

But the Kid didn't ride south, as we know, and in a matter of months he would face Pat Garrett for the last time.

"He'll steal anything he can get his hands on."

I'd heard Casimiro condemned so often for his "taking ways." As he sat beside me then I looked to my pony that was munching the nearby grass. Casimiro's horse was close by, also nibbling at the new juicy grama. There were a few things fixed to my saddle that might be tempting—and were easily removable—things that could whet the criminal impulse of Casimiro: a new lariat rope; a thirty-thirty carbine in its scabbard, the latter a nice hand-stamped piece of leatherwork I had purchased at Edd Amonett's; and a pair of pliers for fence repair in a holder of its own. And a good yellow "Fish Brand" saddle slicker was rolled and tied behind the cantle. The bridle and reins could be slipped from my pony in a jiffy, and even the horse himself with saddle and all led away should the notorious villan knock me out with a rock.

And the Yaqui had had an outlaw's look to him. . . .

But when I looked away from my horse, I saw that Casimiro had leaned back, put his hat over his face to shade it from sun and flies, and prepared himself for a nap. The clean high-altitude air, the hush undisturbed except for a bird trill or two; the peace of it, had made me drowsy, too. So I leaned back and joined Casimiro in what was probably no more than an hour's rest.

When I awoke, lo and behold! My pony was still grazing, alone. Casimiro and his horse, his stock whip and his nasty thieving desires were gone, perhaps to frighten the women of Richardson, and send them to shelter behind closed doors. Hastily, I made my way to the grazing pony to find every removable saddle fixture in place—carbine, fence pliers, rope, slicker, bridle, even the Navajo saddle blanket.

After that, I saw Casimiro riding his familiar trails, but only from a distance, and tales of his villainy continued to entertain. Then, in the autumn, Bug Merchant came by to ask my help on a job at the ranch, one that would last but a few days, a week at the most. Before leaving I baked a pan of biscuits and boiled a pot of beans, to be there should some rider stop by my lone cabin and care to "stay all night." Padlocks were unknown in those happy years, my door was always open.

On my return I found that someone *had* stopped by. Someone *had* enjoyed a meal of cold beans and biscuits, and the molasses jar had been attacked. Who that someone was didn't matter, for a gift of simple hospitality makes the blood tingle with satisfaction. I would receive the same in any other house. It was the way of the ranch country. I went to the table where next to the kerosene lamp was my pad and pencils, pen and ink bottle. And the guest who partook of my beans and biscuits had left a note! It was done in a hand I had seen before, a piece of writing similar to one that would grace the portal of an Islamic mosque in Aleppo—*Amigo*.

I looked to the walls where hats and clothing and riding accessories hung on nails driven into the logs. I rushed to a trunk without a lock, where what few valuables I owned were stored.

Everything was in place, not a solitary object taken away.

Viva la Amistad!

GUS

Eight
Cowboy Riding Christmas

A ride with Bob Hale in his mail car over the Spindle Route back in the late 1920s, and early 30s, was an excursion into memories of events and places of years past. The route started at Capitan, in Lincoln county, and served boxes along the north side of the Capitan Mountains for some twenty-five miles, the terminus being the abandoned Spindle community.

There was a box at the Stacy Place where two ruts called a road took off north to White Oaks; another at Encinoso; another at the Block Ranch. Next came Richardson, named for the Block foreman who gave Billy the Kid a pony after the escape from Lincoln in 1881. Las Tablas, where the outlaw had a blacksmith relieve his legs of already severed irons. Every foot of the Spindle Route once played a part in converting a quiet landscape of grass, mountain, juniper and pine, and long lonely horizons, into Lincoln county, historically the wildest and wooliest of the nineteenth-century West.

Forlorn along the way were abandoned homestead shacks and cabins, once the homes of sodbusters out of Texas, Oklahoma and points east, who had filed their hundred-sixty-acre claims, dreamed their dreams and broke the furrows, while the smoke that drifted from their chimneys gave incense to faith in the land, hope that the new-found soil which the law called theirs would insure prosperity for generations to come. It was an agricultural heaven in the shadow of the peaks.

They came in the years before, during, and following World War I. They brought their livestock, and rocked in the covered wagons were their wives and progeny, their few possessions and a huge supply of trust. They filed, they felled logs; they built their cabins and put rain water into cisterns from pitched roofs; they split piñon and juniper firewood to warm their new-found wealth; they gave their all by the sweat of the brow. And then, after five or six years, as was the time allotted most of them, they loaded their wagons and moved away, abandoning their log walls and furrowed dreams to the early frosts and drought-laden winds—to the bleaching, unforgiving sun.

Unforgiving, too, were the operators of cattle ranches in the vicinity, long established with a sharp dislike for any upstart arrived to disturb the rich grama grass turf and convert it to patches of pinto beans and corn. But, while the homesteaders toiled and battled, their thoughts were on a tight little community of themselves, shelter and sustenance for their womenfolks, even a short elementary education for the children—short, no further than the fourth grade, for the Mountain View community wanted no educated fools in its midst.

So they built a one-room schoolhouse, a rough frame affair with a bell—and, they named it Mountain View. It sat beside the Capitan-Spindle road at the foot of Dry Canyon. The kids attended for the duration, then it, too, was emptied, along with abandonment of their homes. To show their contempt for the folk who built it the area cowboys dubbed it "Hog Wallow." And they left it alone, except for holding cattle-business-meetings, at times, as a polling place every election year—and for joyous celebration in the starlight of Christmas Eve.

The warmth of its pot-belly stove was revived, tinsel decorations hung about and a pine-needle bouquet nailed to the door. And there to the tune of fiddle, jew's harp and harmonica the birthday of a Child born long ago in an equally squalid run-down atmosphere was observed as the whole Christian world paid like homage to the Event. While the Cowboy's Christmas Hoe-Down wore notches in the rough-pine floor, bootheels pounding and the daintiest of print skirts in fashion swirling in the light of stable lanterns. Revelry and cheer was the order of the night, for a lonely mountain setting was dedicated to peace and good will, when grudges were temporarily forgotten.

"That there's Hog Wallow," Bob Hale would explain in broad daylight to a mail car passenger, while he stopped his Chevrolet at the Block Ranch mail box. "Ain't nothin' inside no more. But we whooped it up there last Christmas. Maybe we didn't wallow, but we sure went *pure* hog-wild."

The ranch bunkhouse of fifty or sixty years ago was a dreary domicile indeed, 100 percent masculine, the occupants disdainful of any phase of life that had frills or "fooferaw" attached. A special dislike was dressing up and "putting on the dog" for foreign occasions—like Christmas.

But where children were about, that was a different breed of critter, because Christmas was "kids' stuff" anyway. A tree decorated with tinsel could actually be found in some of the ranch houses, with gifts wrapped and labeled beneath the lower limbs. A "kid's saddle" new and unscratched from Amonett's saddlery in Roswell, or a set of bridle and bits from S. D. Myres in El Paso, or silver-mounted Kelly spurs from Porter's in Tucson. Or maybe a pretty card saying how a new saddle pony was waiting for a little rider out in the corral, gentled and broken to cow work, just right for junior who would develop bow legs before the age of eight.

As recently as fifteen years ago an aged and "stove-up" cowboy inquired of the postmistress in a very small southwestern New Mexico town the procedure of sending a Christmas card. He confessed he was "plumb greenhorn" about Christmas cards, but he had an old partner in Texas, aged and stove-up as himself, who'd ridden on many a roundup with him, shared bunkhouses and trail-camps, "helled around" in the cow towns and rode chuck line together—"who would be right proud to know how his old side-kick in New Mexico was gittin' along."

The postmistress advised him to find the drug store in Lordsburg, select a card of his choice from many on the rack, sign his name below the greeting, bring it to her and she'd mail it off to Texas. A few days later the old cowpoke showed up with his purchase, a truly sentimental reminder of long-ago brotherhood, a card printed in lavender on a background of soft grey, bordered with a tone of crinoline and lace, appropriate for the pleasure of someone in the twilight of life, be that life ever so alkalied, bowlegged, wind-blasted and sun-blistered, a greeting to bring tears of emotion—a greeting undersigned with affection. And the greeting read—

Merry Christmas, Dear Grandmother.

Away from the lighted ranch-houses where the season's joy was rampant in childish anticipation, in the adult delight of wrapping gifts and preparation for a family feast that only the Joy of Joys would induce the womenfolks to prepare, out there in the tobacco-smoked bunkhouses, or high in the saddle with feel of the lariat on work-calloused hands, amidst the bawl of cattle and nicker of horses, out there on the winter-browned baldies. There the spirit of Scrooge rode the range—Christmas! Humbug! Fooferaw!

Perhaps the true sense of the meaning of Christmas fifty years ago was in the valleys, high in the mountains or on the plains of *Spanish* New Mexico.

The adobe churches, the blazing fires that gave light to the entrances, words of joy and good will spoken in the most lilting language of any in the world, the perfume of burning piñon, the midnight feasts of *posole*, purely New Mexican cakes and goodies, families and friends and neighbors together. And out by their tents on the range, *los pastores*, the humblest of men who tended the sheep—*and there were in the same country shepherds abiding in the field, keeping watch over their flock by night*. For they in the canyons of Socorro, on the high plains of San Miguel and Harding, there was no *posole*, no *empanadas de fruta*, no *biscochitos* tasty with anise. But if the night was clear, there was a star.

As the 1920s drifted into the 30s, I lived in a cabin on the north side of the Capitan mountains, idling and writing, working short jobs on the local ranches as opportunities arose. So when the Christmas season arrived I was blessedly content.

A family of homesteaders lived nearby who by their friendship, tenacity and veracity had a strong hold on my admiration. Their house was a one-room log affair heated by a cast-iron cookstove. They drew rain water in buckets from a cistern. And, as they were strongly averse to "puttin' on the dog," clothing was for comfort, never for show. They lived on a never-changing year-long diet of pinto beans boiled in hog-grease, corn-pone of their own field-growing and hand-grinding, fried potatoes, and Arbuckle's coffee because it was the cheapest. And in spite of it all, the family motto could have been "*What more would Christian people want?*" They had arrived two years before in a covered wagon from the Oklahoma Ozarks.

One day as December moved to a close, I had a horseback rider pull up at my place. "Day after tomorrow is Christmas, ain't it?" he asked, with a sort of happy grin on his face.

"You're right," I said. "Thursday."

"Paw and Maw says you'all eat Christmas dinner with us. Maw's gonna bake. Do you like pie?"

Did I love pie! Does any batching bachelor love pie! Apple, mince, pumpkin, any kind. So after I convinced the rider that I loved pie, he rode off trailing dust toward the homestead shack a mile away.

Which gave me a happy thought. A relative had sent me a small Christmas check in a letter brought in by Bob Hale's mail car a few days before. I was aware of the nature of the festive pie, to be served along with the corn-pone, fried potatoes and beans—a special pie, a treat for Christmas day. So I made plans to saddle up and ride into Capitan, fifteen miles across The Gap, and bring home a gunnysack half-full of holiday tasties that I knew the homesteaders had never sampled in all their rustic lives. I couldn't have thought of a better way to spend the Christmas gift that was snug in my wallet.

The morning of Christmas Eve found me in Titsworth's store, asking Mr. Provine to hand me down a canned ham from the shelf, or maybe a couple while he was about it. And a fruit cake, pound boxes of chocolates and a dozen bags of assorted candies, some were soft to the chew with real jawbusters mixed in for exercise. I saw a can of shrimp temptingly set beside a jar of mayonnaise, which along with pimentos and chopped onion would make a nice salad—and a head of lettuce that would fit just right in my gunnysack. And bakery stuff, doughnuts and cinnamon rolls, fine company for the fruit cake. Shiny-gold oranges and ripe-red apples, a couple loaves of "light bread" that I thought might relieve the monotony of corn-pone. And then, as a kind afterthought, I decided on gifts for the old man and his lady—a spank-new sunbonnet and about a week's supply of Brown's Mule chew tobacco. The two grown sons could share the latter. There were no small children in the family.

The sun shone bright on Christmas morning after a clear sky had starlit Christmas Eve. At noon I proudly rode to the homestead shack. The loaded gunnysack tied behind the cantle bounced cheerily to the trot of the pony. But suddenly a thought came to me that suggested I might be wasting good intention. Perhaps I could have better spent my money some other way. My dinner host, as he had stressed upon me many times before, had been the village blacksmith back in the Ozarks. He had also served as the village dentist. His specialty, then, was pulling teeth. A not-so-sanitary pair of mechanic's pliers sat on the bench along with the tongs, sledge, farrier and ball peen hammers.

"Didn't it hurt?" I asked him, once, when he recalled an extra-tough case of molar pulling.

For a reply I got a look of hate. For time and again he impressed on me his disgust for any human who would wince with pain when a tooth was yanked from his gums, some half-a-man who would patronize "one of them there sissy-prissy fellers in white coats along Roswell Main Street." For an anesthetic and stanching of blood, Paw's men patients were given a hunk from a braid of chew tobacco, a dip of Copenhagen for the womenfolks.

Then how, I wondered as I loped toward my dinner, would such a host feel toward a guest bearing a gift of fruit cake?

"Mountain Home" was the name for the interior of that cabin. The cast-iron cookstove warmed the log walls to perfection, walls decorated with a shotgun and a rifle each on its separate set of hooks, and four trophy deer antlers nailed at the cardinal points. The oil-clothed table was ready for the feast, plates set, and cups rim-down waiting for Arbuckles. On a shelf near the cookstove sat a shaving mug and strop-razor that served the men, and from a nail hung a towel sufficient for all. Conspicuous was a bottle of Ziegel's Essence, a product of the Tennessee hill country, the contents black with the consistency of tar, a purgative so volcanic in action that a tablespoonful mixed in a cup of hundred-proof home-stilled whiskey would not only put ruts in the trail to the backhouse but the very thought of it frightened the revenue agents away. The ghostly form of a large canvas-covered object occupied a corner of the room, which I knew to be a whiskey still.

The little family stood at the table, tempted by what I may have had in the gunnysack—and, wisely, I pulled out a bag of oranges first.

They all beamed with delight.

Then the apples. The nuts, the whole assortment of walnuts, brazil and pecans. The sunbonnet for Maw and the Brown's Mule for Paw and the boys.

And Lord, were they tickled to death!

Then—and I shudder for the memory—I reached in and brought out the canned ham.

"What in hell is that there?" Paw said.

"It's a ham in a can."

I watched the scowls as I placed the fruit cake gingerly on the table, followed by the mayonnaise and one can of shrimp. Knowing that a can opener was an instrument never to be tolerated in *that* household I brought one along and with all the courage I could muster applied it to the can of shrimps.

"Git them maggots out of here!" Paw hollered, while Maw and the boys sought sanctuary in the vicinity of the whiskey still. They all eyed me with distrust. They kept their distance from the fruit cake as though it was a coiled rattlesnake. The candy was received as so much fooferaw—and when I emptied the little sack of chocolate droplets, each drop the size of a pinto bean, Paw asked me what sheep corral I had been working around lately.

"Git that truck out of here!" he shouted, pointing a calloused hand at my kind intention spread on the table. "Pack it in your sack and hang it out on a tree. But you can leave us the apples and the nuts. Then you can come set with Christian folks and have some dinner. Maw baked a pie—four pies, enough for us all."

So we enjoyed a Christmas feast of fried potatoes, corn-pone, Arbuckles and pinto beans—beans, the Great Bean of the great Southwest! And when Maw proudly placed a pie on the table—lo and behold, it was *bean pie*—mashed pintos with sugar, raisins, and cinnamon mixed in, a festive dish if any deserved the compliment. And while we dined with Paw recalling old days in the Ozarks, I thought of all the canned ham and oranges, shrimp salad on lettuce, fruit cake and assorted candies I would enjoy in my solitude for days to follow.

I recall now how the Spirit of Santa Claus joyously arrived at the north side of The Gap of the Capitans a couple Christmases after that gala celebration. There was a couple ranching nearby, native New Mexicans both, of whom I was very fond. I became acquainted with them as newlyweds a few years before on the Diamond A Ranch, and we remained fast friends ever since. Now there were children added to the household, and seven or eight hound dogs of sundry colors and dispositions. My neighbor rode into the mountains with his hounds to track down predators on the complaints of ranchers who had stock grazing the timber. The offenders were mostly mountain lions, and he was probably the most expert lion hunter in New Mexico.

When that very special Christmas was in the planning stage, a week or so before the actual Eve, my neighbor asked if I would do the family a favor, especially so the children, by dressing up and playing Santa Claus.

"I know where you can get a red coat, a cap with a tassel on it, and white whiskers to cover your face," he encouraged.

It seemed that a complete Santa Claus costume could be found on loan at the extensive Merchant Ranch a couple miles to the west at the foot of Gum Spring Canyon. Lon Merchant had purchased it some years before for the Christmas Eve entertainment of his three little daughters and two younger nephews. But now the daughters and nephews were past the Santa Claus stage. The outfit rested in a closet as a memento only.

Lon graciously pulled it out of the mothballs when I asked for the loan—shiny knee-high black boots, baggy red pants, a red fur-trimmed jacket three times my size, a tasseled cap and a wig of flowing locks that was part of it, and enough white stick-on beard to disguise any face no matter how familiar.

"We have the gifts in a sack," my neighbor explained, planning strategy while the kids were out of the way. It was the afternoon of Christmas Eve, no less. "You've got the outfit, now maybe you can use this," he added, handing me a brass bell with a loud clapper, taken off a bell mare or a cow of his out on the pasture.

The plan was that I take the sacked gifts to my place, dress up in the Santa Claus costume, then just at dusk approach the mountain home, the sack over my shoulder, ringing the bell, loudly calling "Ho, ho, ho!" The whole family would be there at the door to greet me, and after a joyful distribution of presents my reward was to enjoy a supper of fried chicken with all its holiday fixings. And be assured, the children had been coached beforehand on how to carry on a conversation with Santa Claus.

I wrapped a light army blanket around my waist for added girth. The sack over my shoulder was bulky but not heavy, and the bell rang cheerily in the crisp winter twilight air. A low ridge lay ahead of my plodding path, one topped with a growth of pine. The ruts called a road cut a gap between two arboreal majesties of the forest dark against the sky. About an eighth of a mile beyond the piney ridge was the ranch-house, where the children would be anxiously awaiting my arrival.

Now I reached the summit, to behold the lighted windows and open door, with the entire family standing ready to greet me. They cried a welcome—the culminating moment to weeks of childish anticipation, little hands held over hearts beating in rapture, eyes wide with wonder—the time was now! Now when Santa Claus would descend the slope, sack over shoulder, bell ringing joyously, jolly old Saint Nick loudly crying, "Ho, ho, ho!" Christmas Eve, when all the good boys and girls on this ranch were eager for the presents in my sack. "Ho, ho, ho! . . . Get ready, kids, because here comes Santa Claus!"

They saw me, the dear little bullet-heads and moppets. They danced with glee, clapping their tiny hands. They saw me on the ridge, they screamed for joy—

But the hound dogs saw me, too. They barked and bayed, and took off in my direction ready to bring down a panther.

I dropped the sack and the bell went clanging to the ground, for almost upon me were the seven or eight baying hounds, their fangs bared, fire in their eyes. The grounded sack spilled toys and goodies, a rag doll, little boxes done up in Christmas wrapping and frosty tinsel.

A pine trunk rose to the sky about six feet from my stand of terror, its lowest limb well above my reach.

I never was too athletic, and tree climbing was an exercise I could happily do without. But the snarling canines, almost frothing at the mouth, were a few short feet from my polished black boot, intent on ripping the drooped seat of my Santa Claus pants.

To climb the tree to safety was humanly impossible; that is, under ordinary circumstances. But sheer terror can play lifesaving tricks. For just as an infuriated set of teeth was about to take first grip of my leg, I found myself going up that trunk as though it were a graveled track—a familiar way to sanctuary. Holding fast to a limb I looked down upon my tormentors that were barking and snarling below, ravenous for my flesh. The good neighbor and wife hurried toward my perch, ready to call off the hounds.

A shout—a command—and the well-trained pack quit baying and sat like canine gentlemen. A welcome silence overtook the scene—blessed Holy Night silence.

Until the small piping voice of little T. J., looking up at me, inquired—"How big are you, Santa Claus?"

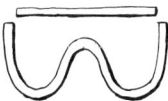

Nine
Song of the Saddlemen

Back in earlier times, some fifty or more years ago, the working day of a Southwestern cowboy was often one of summer-scorched solitude or winter-numbed loneliness, a day that stretched from the rise of the morning star to the last faint glow of sundown. Sometimes there was little to do, riding alone to scan the prairie and leave undisturbed the cattle that grazed the tawny stretches toward the skyline.

 A slow walk or easy trot was all that was required of the pony, a dismount at times to stretch the limbs and cool the saddle, to roll a smoke while the mount dragged bridle reins to nibble at some grassy tidbit. And maybe hum or whistle a tune—or sing a cheery stanza from *The Cowboy's Dance Song*, or something tender like *The Lovesick Cowboy*, or, if the mood was right, a mournful lament like *The Streets of Laredo*. But whatever the words or the tune, it would be a *cowboy* song—saddleman from silver-mounted spurs to high felt Stetson.

 Other days would be filled with action. Hard riding over high baldies or alkali sinks, up and down or across arroyos, on the trail drive or at the roundup. The cowboy would find all the company a man could ask for there—the wagon boss himself, the cook and his potrack, the wranglers tending the remuda.

 It was work brutal on the human constitution, although some might call the scene colorful. Dust and bellowing and nickering, shouting, and whistling. And aimed at the livestock was the most frightful category of oaths. Not a trace of romance anywhere. Nothing musically tender, just a song wild and reckless, although Hollywood often has the boys riding hoof-worn trails as strains of Vivaldi come softly from behind the rocks.

The song of the day was the branding iron. And the castration knife, and the vaccine syringe, the lariat rope and its hold on the saddle horn. The roper at work, the tightened loop dragging unbranded calves to the fire of red-hot coals, to a pair of flankers and the man with the iron. There's the bawl of a creature in agony when the brand is applied, and the knife put to surgery, converting little bulls into little steers, and the ear marked with an officially recorded crop, split, or swallow fork for further identification. There's the gathered herd, milling about or standing in awe at the antics of the human species. There'd be changing of horses throughout the day, roping fresh mounts out from the remuda. Strain and sweat, a tax on the eyes and a jab at every muscle of the body.

And then—sundown. The fiery horizon glow turns the prairie to amethyst, the off-yonder mountains to gray or cobalt. What mountains? The Capitans, likely, or the San Mateos, or Pajarito Peak. What prairie? Maybe the cedar-braked, arroyo-gutted flats north or south of the Gallo, or east of Rabenton Draw, or amid the sacahuista hills down by the Rio Feliz—anywhere that's cowboy riding country.

Mounted men in double-rigged saddles are stationed around the herd, which they'll hold to graze into and through the night—likewise the horse wranglers keeping tight the remuda. And while the sun gives the world over to night, the blaze of the cook's potrack fire, up against the wagon, gives an invite to all who can—to rest, to dine, to stretch out on his own horse-sweaty bed of canvas tarp and soogans. To talk fool-talk.

And if some old boy has a *French harp* (harmonica) in his warbag, then a couple fellers might take time to sing a song—a cowboy song, one more history than harmony, maybe the long monotonous chant of *When the Work's All Done This Fall*, or *Jesse James*, or *Bury Me Not on the Lone Prairee*. But whatever, it would recount in nasal tones the wild days along long-ago trails, stampedes and bucking horses, outlaws, saloons, famous sheriffs, or brave or cowardly cowboys. Or, if the songsters were in a mellowed mood, they might voice the sad ditty of *Brown-Eyed Lee*.

We all know how Lee's lover sold his cattle and corn, all to win her wedding vow—and bought a license, and how his name was Red. But Brown-Eyed Lee's mother packed a six-shooter and threatened to kill Red dead in his tracks if he ever again approached her daughter. So Red saw no hope for his loving attentions. He sold his horse and saddle and caught the northbound train. And what did a broken-hearted lover do when the train dropped him off at the depot? Well, he went to the pool hall to shoot a game of billiards.

But every click of the ball echoed the maidenly voice of Brown-Eyed Lee. Yet, sadly, there was always the vision of the hellcat mother, so with satisfaction Red sang: *Although I'm broken-hearted, there's one thing I know well, that the one who caused this bust-up will someday scorch in hell.*

The listeners would sip Arbuckle's coffee in the light of the cook's fire, while a few tired hands dozed off to sleep on their canvas tarps. Even the granite-hearted cook would suffer along with Red, gulping at times with emotion, as a love song bathed the roundup camp with tenderness, injecting romance, such as it was, into one of the most unromantic scenes on earth.

The cowboy of southern New Mexico in general is the exact replica of the "good old boys" of Texas—morally, physically, emotionally, and spiritually. Life on the range some 50 years ago was one of ever-present danger, and courage and determination were demanded of the cowboy by the boss, plus a thorough knowledge of the ways of the cattle and horses, the former animals usually stupid and the latter fractious. To hold his job, meager as the wages were, he had to prove his ability—otherwise he'd be fired. The industry prospered on the work of an intelligent rider astride a sensible, manageable horse. There were "bucking broncs" in most horse pastures and just as many "no count" cowboys in the bunkhouse. Neither proved a credit to a working ranch.

There were two distinct breeds. One was the cowboy who had, by grace of good ranch family upbringing, obtained sufficient education to instill an ambition to "block up" a livestock enterprise of his own, engage in community affairs, marry and bring to the West little facsimiles of his bowlegged self. Clean thinking, morally upright, maybe a little self-righteous in the presence of women, far more human when riding the pastures, in the corral, or next to the cook's roundup potrack.

The other type of rangehand was the "tramp" cowboy, a man whose wealth consisted of his saddle, bridle, and bits, saddle blanket, slicker, chaps, and spurs, the clothes on his back, the boots on his feet, and the hat atop his head. And the contents of his warbag—perhaps a change of shirt and longhandles. The ever-familiar bedroll wrapped in canvas and bound with rope. Two or three lariats, maybe a .30-.30 saddle gun in a scabbard. Possibly a couple ponies of his own, convenient when out of a job and riding chuck line.

And his greatest wealth of all—an unfettered perpetual bachelor, free to ride the West, to labor or loaf at will, to live his days in his own style among his own kind. To be clannish, brutish if such was necessary, generous, kind without showing emotion, loyal to his employer and vocation. To express anathema for all that is sensitive and gentle, especially the blessing of schools and their teachers and all manner of sissified pursuits.

"I ain't got no education," bragged a bunkhouse companion back in 1926, "but I know cows from A to Z." I inquired, but never learned, which end of the cow was A and which Z.

Yet it was one of the West's most educated and respected cowboys who composed the song of the range foremost in popularity, lauded by the saddlemen as their own and their pride: *It's little Joe the wrangler, he'll wrangle nevermore, for his days with the remuda, they are o'er.*

The song goes on to tell of a young rider out of Texas, who appears in roundup camp mounted on a pony named Chaw, *with his brogan shoes and overalls, a tougher lookin' kid you never in your life before had saw.* Every cowboy present took an immediate liking to the boy, and the wagon boss gave him a job with the remuda, *learned him to wrangle horses and try to know them all, and get them in by daylight if he could, to follow the chuck wagon and always hitch the team, and help the cocinero rustle wood.*

But Little Joe the Wrangler's time with the horse herd was of brief duration, for on reaching the Pecos River, a violent lightning storm sent the herd into a stampede, like *a hailstorm long they fled, and we were all aridin' for the lead.* And where in the commotion was Little Joe? *He was ridin' old Blue Rocket with a slicker o'er his head, atryin' to check the cattle in their speed.* At last, when the stampede was stopped and the cattle brought to milling, the cowboys found one of their crew to be missing. *The next morning just at daybreak, we found where Rocket fell, down a washout some 20 feet below. And beneath the horse mashed to a pulp—his spur had rung his knell—was our little Texas stray, poor Wrangler Joe.*

N. Howard (Jack) Thorp was a New Mexico cowboy—a Carrizozo, Capitan, Lincoln County cowboy—and he was the composer of the tragedy of Little Joe. Jack Thorp was born in New York City in June 1867, the son of a wealthy, prominent lawyer. He spend his boyhood with the upper crust of New York and Philadelphia and Newport, educated at the exclusive St. Paul's School, going on to Princeton, where he earned a degree in civil engineering.

Ever looking to the West, he moved to Nebraska, where in partnership with his brother and Marshall Field II of Chicago, he started a ranch on the Platte. But in 1886, at age nineteen, Jack found himself at Kingston in the Black Range working for his cousin Frank Underwood at his Enterprise Mine.

Later he cowboyed in Texas, then back to New Mexico and the Block Ranch north of the Capitans and the Bar W by the Carrizozo malpais.

All the while, he was writing books—something not to be trusted by the strictly unlettered set in the bunkhouse. It was his fellow writer, the great Eugene Manlove Rhodes, who described Jack Thorp as one of the ablest cowboys and daring bronc riders he had ever known. Thorp composed *Little Joe the Wrangler* in 1898, and it was published in a book of songs in Estancia some years later. He spent his last years in a house beside the highway in Alameda, north of Albuquerque, a simple rustic adobe in his day—now modernized and stuccoed over like most of Jack Thorp's West.

By this time out at the roundup camp, they have completed the rendition of *Brown-Eyed Lee* and perhaps given the cook a treat with *Little Joe the Wrangler*. There were hundreds of cowboy songs "written down" through the frontier years between 1860 and the turn of the century, but one or a couple bowlegged gents could be expected to know perhaps a dozen.

Among the dozen would be the old familiars, such as *The Chisholm Trail* with its seventy-three verses and the chorus of *coma ti yi youpy, youpy yea, youpy yea*. Or, *Goodbye, Old Paint, I'm Leavin' Cheyenne*. Or they might shed a tear because prohibition was the law and conjure fond memories of the days when cowboys could nudge up to the bar rail and order some rye whiskey: *Rye whiskey, rye whiskey, rye whiskey, I cry. If I cain't git rye whiskey I surely will die*. Or of times back when gamblers dealt faro and monte in casinos up and down the streets of Roswell and Carrizozo. When in White Oaks, Madam Varnish glittered in her prime—when the chuck-a-luck cage took more in than it gave out and roulette clicked its merry rounds and the green felt-topped tables shone bright under the harp lamps, and boys with the chips gloated greedily over a card called—the Jack O'Diamonds: *Jack O'Diamonds, Jack O'Diamonds, I know you from old, for you've robbed my poor pockets of silver and gold*.

And what about the girls in Emma's in Roswell, or Billie Dee's in Carrizozo, or Marie's in Alamogordo? Didn't those little sweetnesses deserve a toast? Sex and violence, jealousy and unbridled intemperance were as rampant in the song of the saddlemen as on television today. So a stanza or two of *Lulu* wouldn't be out of line: *My Lulu hugged and kissed me, she wrung my hand and cried, she said I was the sweetest thing that ever lived or died*.

Lulu was never one for the cares of motherhood. *My Lulu had twin babies, they was born on Christmas Day; she bust one's head with the rollin' pin, but the other got away.* And she was "right smart fond of likker." *My Lulu is a dandy, she drinks whiskey like a man; she calls for gin and brandy, and she don't give a damn.* She incited violent possessiveness in the heart of her lover. *So don't you monkey with my Lulu gal, or I'll tell you what I'll do; I'll slice you with my bowie knife and shoot you through and through.*

When the sky was blackened and the fire wore down to simmering coals, long after the voices and French harp were silenced for the night, and when the stars alone gave light to the bedded-down herd, that's when the night guards sat their saddles or walked their ponies softly, gently round and about the sleeping or cud-chewing cattle. That's when they gave a song to the loneliness of the scene. A lullaby, maybe, or a lament or a drone, just to let the cattle know that the cowboys were present. The voice was an act of precaution, for range cattle are easily spooked. A rider without song could move close to a sleeping cow, wake her into frenzy, and send commotion through the herd, resulting in a stampede. The songs were of the soft, lilting kind— *When You and I Were Young, Maggie,* and *Silver Threads Among the Gold.*

I remember a ranch bunkhouse I shared with others for a 12-month period in the mid-1920s. It was a dark domicile, rock-walled inside and out, the floor of concrete and the ceiling low and cobwebby. Light entered by a small window at the north, the sash held up by a broken Colt .45 Frontier model revolver with a wooden grip—an attempt to admit even a paucity of fresh air to the stale cigarette smoke, tobacco spit-scented interior.

Center of the room was a wood-burning, cast-iron stove, the rusty tin pipe zigzagging to the roof, a thing of warmth and comfort spat at a thousand times for good luck. There was a small table for the blackjack and poker players. No chairs, but half-a-dozen nail kegs with gunnysack seats that served the purpose. A coal-oil lamp with a sooted chimney in the center of the table. Any wall decoration would be held in contempt by the occupants, but for a practical purpose large nails were driven at intervals into the chinked walls from which hung hats, slickers, chaps (pronounced shaps), lariats, every imaginable accessory of the saddle—bridles, spurs, an occasional pair of pants, and drooped fabrics that were jackets and shirts.

Around the room, closer to the stove in winter, were the beds of the ranch hands—layers of blankets and quilts sandwiched on the floor between an under and upper cover of canvas tarp. The nearest washbasin was on a stand a hundred yards away, at the door of the cookshack. The roller towel by the basin was usually black and slick, a change to pristine white occurring about every two weeks.

On trips to Roswell about every three or four weeks, we patronized the barber shop at the corner of Second and Main. On warm summer days we bathed more frequently in the Rio Hondo, about a half-mile from the bunkhouse.

Idle hours in the bunkhouse would have been insufferably dull had it not been for the three or four grimed decks of cards, some worn-out copies of *Western Stories*, *Lariat*, and *Ace High* magazines, the constant talk of horses and assorted cowboys, and of neighboring or far away ranches that paid better wages, maybe five dollars more a month. And practical jokes, such as hiding items of saddlery, or the saddle blankets we brought in to serve as pillows after turning the ponies loose—simple humor that produced hearty guffaws.

And the thick cigarette smoke above and around the poker table, and the prone bodies stretched on the canvas beds, heads on folded saddle blankets, each with its individual man-odor, hollering smart talk across the room, or maybe in chorus rendering a song-ballad of the wide-open, sun-blessed, lonely, sad, or raucously humorous West.

One would lead off with a first stanza, a half-dozen others carrying on, and the cowboy world in harmony and words would shine in the close lamplit room—wild stampedes as they were sung in *Utah Carroll*, the pathetic days of the homesteader as recalled in *Greer County*, the roughest of living described in *The Little Old Shanty on My Claim*, the wild bucking bronc in *The Zebra Dun*, outlaws like *Sam Bass*. Or: *Come all you Texas cowboys, and warnin' take from me. Don't go up to Montana to spend your money free. But stay at home in Texas, where work is all year round, and you'll never catch consumption from sleepin' on the ground.*

And so the saddle songs ranged the West through the simple, carefree times of fifty years ago. Until the tunes changed as the lifestyle of the cowboy began to conform to the ways of a society so alien to his own—and the voice rang over the airwaves to the accompaniment of guitars rendered by big-hatted, booted, bearded, and spangled men, who were not cowboys at all, but performers who sold record albums and signed million-dollar contracts, and who never knew the loneliness, the grueling hardships, the ever-present danger, and the exquisite joys and freedom that fired the blood and mind of the old-time cowboy.

Long, long ago the Spanish Longhorn was replaced on the range with

English Hereford and Scottish Shorthorn and Angus—and more lately the East Indian Brahma and the French Charolais, as the old scrub-oak-and-cedar fire that once heated the branding irons has been surrendered to propane. And long gone is the horse herd that once followed the roundups, now given to horse trailers and the beds of pickup trucks—for the saddle horse is not so much the necessity he was, and the bunkhouses are now blessed—or cursed—with television, its sound replacing the songs of the real and the true. Cowboy wages are no longer thirty-five or forty dollars a month, and no more do they ride chuck line from ranch to ranch when looking for employment, for even the hospitality of the old West is gone out of fashion, never to be again.

Back before the turn of the century the change could be felt coming on, just as surely as the morning star timed the start of the saddleman's day. And on a dark and starry night, maybe somewhere beyond the Caprock, a slow-riding night guard sang lullaby to a bedded-down herd, gave reprimand to a steer, which in his own bovine way perhaps knew life and freedom would end at the shipping pens beside the long train of cattle cars somewhere ahead and bawled a show of defiance as the saddleman gave his own prediction with a song from his heart:

> Hushaby, Longhorn,
> Your pards are all sleepin',
> Quit your durn millin'
> And tossin' your head,
> Wavin' your horns,
> So unrestful and sweepin',
> All of the beef herd
> With eyes big and red.
> Maybe you know while
> You're pawin' the dust up,
> Bellerin' ugly and swishin' your tail,
> Maybe you know that
> We're nearin' the bust up,
> Nearin' the quittin' place,
> The end of the trail.

Ten
Bad from the Boots Up

Lincoln county, New Mexico. Conjure the name, give it place in the silence of the mind, read a mere mention of it in print, and a vision takes over—a phantom known the world over, revered along the streets of Roswell, filmed in Hollywood, put into song in Nashville, and glorified in the Westerners Corrals of London and Munich.

Not the clean blue skies of the West, the rainwashed meadows of the White Mountains or the aspen summits of the Capitans; not the sootless, untrodden snow-depths where the Jicarillas drop down to Rabenton Draw, or the apple, plum, and peach orchards in bloom on the Hondo or Ruidoso—and most certainly not the tranquil clusters of *paisano* adobes, pure with the color of earth and hewn cedar, blazoned with the presence of an autumn-gold cottonwood.

No indeed, nothing so pastoral or nourishing to the soul. Whisper or think Lincoln county, and a ghost takes over the scene.

Billy the Kid!

The entire American West was "Badman Country" from the 1860s through the 1880s, and every badman was a hoodlum, as the brand fits the breed. The ignorant, unwashed, dusty horseman was everywhere with his "pardner" or his gang. Ford County, Kansas, had its share in Dodge City, likewise Coffeyville. Hangtown, California was so named for its method of retribution—and who can forget Cochise County, Arizona, and the O.K. Corral?

But Billy the Kid was not the only bootful of worthlessness that made Lincoln County famous. There was the Harrell Family—Ben, Sam, Tom and the others—who went around the Hondo and Bonito valleys picking quarrels, entering houses, and killing anyone they thought fit to die. Outlaws were as thick at Seven Rivers and Black River Village as rattlesnakes in the Carrizozo malpais. Cowboys, ranch foremen and land-holding stockmen were numbered among those who sought shelter in New Mexico. They were blooded Texans "wanted" in the beloved homeland by assorted lynch-mobs and hangmen. As late as the 1920s I constantly heard threats offered by cowpokes against someone who offended them. Never did they vow to "beat him up" or "give him a piece of my mind." It was always "I aim to shoot him." One did, and again there were nearly all who didn't.

In all my sixteen-and-a-half years residence in Lincoln county I never saw anyone shot. Once I was close by a couple miles when in the spring of 1927 an old homesteader on the north side of the Capitans went berserk at the Block Ranch mailbox on the Spindle Route. Mounted, he shot and killed Bob White, the forest ranger, who was in a passing automobile. But Pete Johnson, the Lincoln county sheriff, was in the same car—so old Pete just took aim and shot the feisty old mountaineer off his horse. About the same time, "on the wrong side of the tracks" in Roswell, I walked into a crowd that was watching a noted gambler die after being shot by a town law officer. He was dressed like a dude and bleeding profusely. An old-timer who stood beside me said philosophically, "That no 'count gambler got what he needed." On my other side two nuns from St. Mary's Hospital knelt on the ground telling their rosaries and praying for the gambler's soul, wherever it was going. And by the way he writhed and gasped in the dirt it certainly seemed it was going somewhere.

But pioneers were made of granite stuff, and ruthless but thorough were the methods used by honest society in dealing with outlaws. In Lincoln county the sheriffs, marshals and their deputies—Garrett, Poe, McKinney, and a dozen others—were almost as well known as the felons on horseback. Sometimes nuisances were dispatched by a sort of "citizen execution," and nothing more was said about it—except maybe "good riddance."

For example, readers of *The Santa Fe New Mexican* observed in a newsy dispatch in the issue of February 8, 1877, datelined Lincoln, New Mexico:

> At Wiley's cattle camp, some 80 miles below here, about six weeks since, a man named Yopp, in charge of the herd, became enraged at an employee, Buck Powell. He drew his revolver and fired three shots at him. Buck woke up, seized a Winchester and shot Yopp in the mouth, the ball coming out of the back of the neck. Yopp fell and remained for a few moments insensible. Suddenly recovering, he reopened fire on Powell. Powell's gun hung fire. He then seized Yopp's own gun and

shot him through the heart. Powell did not receive a scratch. He wanted to go some 150 miles and give himself up for trial. But was persuaded not to. So the matter ended.

Albuquerque seemed to thrive in the heart of Outlaw Country a hundred years ago and the newspapers gave much space to the crime situation. A reprint from the *Albuquerque Journal* was read by the folks of Cimarron in their *News and Press* on July 21, 1881, just seven days after Pat Garrett put Billy the Kid to rest in Fort Sumner:

> Five rustlers were lynched at a point twenty miles from this city, on Saturday night. It seems that a gang of cattle thieves has been operating quite extensively among the herds on the Rio Puerco, and the herders made up their minds that immediate punishment should be visited upon anyone caught in the act of running off cattle. The five men who were hung were overtaken Saturday evening and had fifteen cattle in their possession. No ceremony was used, the ropes were speedily adjusted, and five cattle thieves are now shoveling coal.

According to the journals of the time the most popular justice on the bench of the great outdoors was Judge Lynch, the perfectionist. *The Red River Chronicle*, of San Lorenzo, New Mexico, on January 6, 1883, reported that, apparently, his performances in Oregon were so superior that learning of them kindled envy in the hearts of vigilantes in the Southwest:

> Oregon is getting rid of horsethieves pretty fast. Some of the leaders were taken off by powder and lead, others danced in the air at the end of a rope, and the rest squealed on one another, so that the gang is pretty well gone to pieces. There is no appeal from the decision of Judge Lynch; he does things to perfection. He ought to have a couple sessions of his court in New Mexico, against horse and cattle thieves.

On one occasion reported by the *Santa Fe New Mexican*, on May 19, 1881, the supporters of Judge Lynch were led to feel that a spare rope could be used with advantage to hang the justice of the bench:

> Twenty-two head of stock were stolen from the Chloride district, in the Black Range. The thieves were finally captured and taken before a justice of the peace in the district. They were fined $45, and the justice took the horses in payment, and turned the thieves loose. The

miners were naturally incensed, and would have lynched the thieves had it not been that the justice appointed a number of special constables to protect the prisoners. A party of miners set out in pursuit, swearing that they would kill them. They may have been stretched ere this, but we have received no intelligence of the sequel of the trial so far. The justice will be arrested for compounding a felony.

Remorse was seldom exhibited by doomed men on the gallows trap or under the hang-tree limb, as such would be a confession to a lack of gallantry. But an exception was made by a no-good follower of Curly Bill Brocius, scourge of Cochise County, Arizona, and the deserts of southwestern New Mexico, and of Old Man Clanton and his gang of outlaws. Again the *News and Press* of Cimarron reported the execution on its front page of July 21, 1881, along with that of the Rio Puerco lynching previously featured:

> On Saturday, in Tucson, Arizona, Thomas Harper, a cowboy, was hanged for the murder of John Talleday, on last September. His demeanor on the scaffold was cool and jaunty. He made no confession, but left a letter to "Curly Bill," a well known desperado, admonishing him to take warning from him and not be too handy with his pistol, and to "stand a heap from a man before you kill him."

The American West was won by human beings of every category and personality, by home seekers and investors; railroad builders and the Irish and Chinese who built the railroads for them; men of insatiable greed, land swindlers; ranchers hungry for more range, more cattle, more profits, who murdered to satisfy their needs; hard-hearted women, thieves, baronesses of the stock-raising and mining industries; and then there were the dusty, unwashed, cattle and horse thieves. Add the thousands of honestly-ambitious settlers who sought only to reap goodness from the land, to build fireside and family and let the brightest sun of all America shine on their achievement, willing to share the wealth of freedom the West offered.

So to protect the interests of empire building, to shelter the lives and properties of the law-abiding, there just had to be town and federal marshals, deputy marshals, detectives, jails and jailers, sheriffs and their deputies, scaffolds complete with gallows and hang ropes, judges and justices, juries; and guns and ammunition of quality and quantity to match or better those of the outlaws. And integrity was necessary, and valor, though some of the elected or appointed law officers did not possess that stamp of character; and they in the annals of Tombstone, Lincoln, Dodge City, El Paso and Socorro are legion.

Here in New Mexico, from the first invasion of the Texan cattlemen to the enactment of the Taylor Grazing Act of 1934, Cowboy Riding Country had been afflicted or blessed by lawmen of both kinds. Within its boundaries in the very early days were those with feet of clay, the no-goods history has ignored. Then there were the brave and honest who will live forever in the cloistered heritage of the West—Pat Garrett, who rid the region of Billy the Kid, and John Poe and Tip McKinney who helped with the chore. There was Captain Saturnino Baca, for whom the Capitan mountains were named, in return for distinguished service to the wildest frontier. Charles Siringo, the nationally-known detective. And many others of dedication and gallantry, archenemies of those who would offend or endanger the pioneers of a decent society.

One such man could be found, occasionally, at the cowboy gathering place on the corner of Second Street and Main, many years ago, in Roswell.

In 1928, a heyday season for the cowboy corner, he was sixty-one. His hair under a moderate-brimmed Stetson hat was as white as the snows above the Mogollon Rim and his mustache trimmed to match. He was stockily built and very strong, well-tailored in a grey businessman's suit. If I remember correctly, I had never seen him without a stogie-cigar held at an angle at the side of his mouth. His eyes were steel grey, squinted somewhat after a lifetime in the sun. When he talked his voice was quiet, soft-spoken. He was a leader of men—as his biographer Frazier Hunt said, "The last of the Great Cowmen."

Captain Burton C. Mossman was then general manager of the huge Diamond A Ranch that headquartered up the Hondo west of town. And he ran a separate outfit of his own, the Turkey Track, east of the Pecos and out on the plains, a sizable stretch of territory in itself. Everyone who knew him addressed him as "Cap," which he took with pride simply because it was cowboy language—and because it was mindful of the greatest, most valorous achievement of his life. The nickname "Cap" followed him everywhere he went, northward where the Bloom Land & Cattle Company had range for him to oversee—near Wagon Mound, around Rocky Ford in Colorado, over the vast ranch and Indian leases the company held in South Dakota.

Burt Mossman was born near Aurora, Illinois, on April 30, 1867. He was Scotch-Irish on both sides of his family, raised and nourished on the covered wagon frontier of the Minnesota-Dakota border; and at age twenty, again after a long covered wagon trip south, he was riding for cowboy wages

on Warren Carpenter's A Bar A ranch near Montecello, New Mexico. That would be under the hot summer sun of 1887. And in time, after Warren Carpenter was killed by lightning, his brother Andy made Burt his foreman. Soon after that he bought the ranch for $3,000, and his mother and brothers came to live there.

Burt was a young man of twenty-six when, in 1893, he took a train to Trinidad, Colorado, via Chicago, and there got acquainted with Frank Bloom and Mahlon Thatcher, a banker and cattleman of Pueblo, a larger town some fifty miles to the north. Both Colorado men had a problem, a big one involving lots of cattle and money. They needed a man with a thorough knowledge of the range and the fearlessness to match. The region in question was the Bloody Basin north of the Verde River in Arizona, a territory as wild and untamable as any in America north or south of the Mexican border. This was the area north of today's Mazatzal Wilderness, geologically and botanically an expanse of peaks and canyons and dropoff precipices clothed with all manner of cholla cactus, catclaw, and jungles of mesquite. Furthermore, the country was then the home of some of the toughest characters ever born for murder and the unforgiving hang rope.

Cattle ranging in that hell-of-hells was lost property indeed. There were twelve thousand wild ones there that Thatcher and Bloom needed rounding up. The Arizona stockman who owned the herd was deeply in debt to both banks, but if brought to market the cattle would pay off the obligation. He was willing to settle if someone could be found with nerve, spine, and sand enough to fit the task—and nobody in all Arizona could be found with the three necessary qualities. Until the bankers, after a short grilling of young Burt Mossman, were convinced that they had found their man.

So Burt went into the Bloody Basin alone. He met with Granville Graybeal, the rancher, who confessed he had tried to get those cattle rounded up, but he just wasn't the man. Burt liked his honesty. Graybeal was sure there were no cowboys in the district who would care to help, and Burt would have to figure that out for himself. Well, Burt did.

North of the Mazatzal stretched the thousand-foot precipice called the Mogollon Rim, below the Long Valley, a geological boundary line that divided the territory into two Arizonas, north and south, each distinct in climate and topography from the other. And north of the Rim, too, was a great ranch, one of the largest in the world, the habitat of the wildest cattle, fractious horses; of magnificent distances, sky and land painted in colors like no other on earth—the dwelling place of hard men of terrible temper, thieves on the loose, cowboys unmatched for excellence in horsemanship and use of the lariat, most if not all eagerly sought by various sheriff's posses and kill-hungry hangmen. The ranch was called the Hashknife Outfit and in its pastures ranged sixty thousand head of cattle. Burt Mossman did not know it then, but someday and soon he would be the emperor of it all.

Well, Granville Graybeal paid off his debt to the Trinidad and Pueblo banks, all right, because Burt and his cowboys, with a wagon and cook, some ponies and shod mules, got the cattle out of the Bloody Basin. And after that he did all sorts of fooling around—in south Arizona, then up in the Hashknife range below the Navajo reservation; way down in Sonora, Mexico, and further south where Sinaloa hits the Pacific coast. Then east across the Sierra Madre to Chihuahua. Fighting intrigue, settling argument by use of quiet tact out of his steel-blue eyes—lots and lots of times with Winchester and six-shooter. Always on horseback—cattle and ponies, bad men and good men, Burt was a match for them all. Then, in 1898, he took over as superintendent of the great and mighty Hashknife. The headquarters were at Joseph City on the Atlantic & Pacific Railroad, eleven miles west of Holbrook, Arizona.

Burt Mossman, right off, found respect for himself with the Hashknife cowboys, and of everyone else in Joseph City—of men who didn't give a damn for another's life or property, shot themselves out of their own lives, or were quietly hanged for their trespasses. The Hashknife was a refuge for the most violent enemies of decent society the West produced, but also the most able cowboys loyal to the Hashknife company interests. And would you believe it, there was a saloon in Joseph City called the *Bucket of Blood!*

Finn Clanton of the Cochise County rustler family had been a Hashknife cowboy. One night he sat peacefully alone in the ranch cook-house when he heard somebody tapping on the door. He got up to greet the visitor, only to face a man aiming a revolver about six feet from his head. The caller pulled the trigger, and the bullet knocked out four teeth and hit the wall after departing through Finn's cheek. As Finn fell to the floor the gunman left the scene thinking he had killed a Clanton, going who knows where, probably to the Bucket of Blood for a shot of Tanglefoot. But Finn wasn't dead. He rolled himself over to a barrel, stuffed his mouth with flour and stanched the blood. He lived to continue a life of lawlessness along with Old Man Clanton, his brothers and Curly Bill, riding out from their pretty ranch on the San Pedro south of Charleston.

Burt stayed with the Hashknife until it was liquidated in 1900. His interests then took him down to Bisbee where he engaged in the meat packing business, treating southern Arizona to good grain-fed beef shipped in from Texas. But he had earned a reputation of fearlessness, honesty, and a passion for getting a job done. Although he had fought in many gunfights had never killed a man. So it was no surprise to anyone that the Governor of Arizona contacted Burt with a proposition. There was a Mexican desperado on the loose, Augustin Chacon, who had killed without mercy all through southern Arizona. There was a $12,000 reward on his head.

So Burt left his business in the hands of his partner, Tovrea, and brought into being the Arizona Rangers, twelve men with himself as captain. They would battle outlaws all over Arizona, along the Utah border north of the Grand Canyon, down the New Mexico line from the Ceniza mountains to the San Bernardino Valley, hunting brigands north of Yuma and up the Colorado River. And the nastiest of the deadliest was the murderer called Agustin Chacon.

No one could say how many people Chacon had killed—one guess was ten, another swore to twenty-nine. He was huge for the part-Indian he was. He fancied himself with a black bushy beard and won the nickname El Peludo, the Hairy One. A few months before Captain Mossman took over his stint of law-and-order, Chacon and his gang held up a gambling hall in Jerome, murdered sheepherders and prospectors, ambushed a stagecoach, and enjoyed skipping away from sheriffs' posses. He crossed over to Sonora with a pack mule or two of loot.

A few years before, he and his *compadres* raided a store in Morenci and hacked to pieces the owner. The Graham County sheriff and posse captured him in a box canyon after shooting him through the lungs. He recovered in the Solomonsville jail, was tried and sentenced to hang. But there was a little *querida* in town who loved Agustin more than life, and she helped him escape. He found sanctuary in his own Mexico. Thereafter his raids and murders in the United States were confined to the border.

Cap's mission was to bring Chacon back from Mexico alive and healthy. The job would be a tricky one. It was unlawful for Cap or any of his force to enter Mexico as a territorial ranger. But as a United States Deputy Marshal he could do so without breaking the law. He decided to enlist the help of two of the worst bandits in Arizona—old Tombstone men, Billy Stiles and Burt Alvord. It seems that sometime before, when Alvord was town marshal of Willcox and Billy Stiles his deputy, he planned a holdup of a Southern Pacific train at Cochise Junction just west of town. The train was carrying $80,000 in gold coin in the express car. Alvord remained in town and Stiles performed the actual dirty work with the help of one Matt Burts.

Stiles and Burts handed the loot over to Alvord in Willcox, and a box of gold coins was buried out by the big Dry Lake. Stiles and another accomplice, Downing, got drunk to celebrate, and made the mistake of paying for their drinks with gold coin that could only have come from the train robbery. Both implicated Alvord—and all three were jailed in Tombstone. But Stiles and Burts, and Downing, were turned loose with the hope that Stiles would lead Wells Fargo agents to the buried treasure. But Stiles gained access to the jail, shot and wounded the jailer, and then freed Alvord. And Burt Alvord, leaving behind a loving wife and buried treasure, escaped across the line into Sonora, taking Stiles with him.

Mossman was sure Alvord would tell the whereabouts of Chacon for a handsome offer. (A Bisbee judge would guarantee Alvord's freedom after a "trial" in Tombstone.) If, of course, Alvord's hideout could be found. And one way to do that would be through Billy Stiles. But where was Stiles? Hiding out somewhere in Sonora, that was sure.

As Cap rode south toward the border from Bisbee he glanced westward to the skies over the Patagonia mountains, south of which was the American headquarters of Colonel Bill Greene's Cattle Company—the mighty two million-acre San Rafael Ranch in Mexico.

Cap continued west to Nogales, the larger border town and railroad gateway to the west coast of Mexico. He boarded a train for Torres, a mining town below Hermosillo, there to take the branch line to the British-owned Minas Prietas mine. A report told that Billy Stiles had a half-brother working there. And yes, the half-brother knew the whereabouts of Burt Alvord, who in turn knew the hiding place of Billy Stiles.

The English mine superintendent was most gracious. He offered Cap a conveyance, a four-mule wagon with driver. Early in the morning they set off to meet the half-brother. They found the lesser Stiles operating a pump in the hills, one that furnished water for the smelter. The reception was hostile, but after reading Judge Barnes' letter to Alvord, the outlaw's half-brother simmered down, told Cap where Alvord was hiding and even furnished him a horse and saddle. Late that afternoon Mossman faced Alvord in front of a rock *choza*, or hut.

Burt Alvord was full of suspicion, but again the judge's letter changed his attitude. Cap told the fugitive that his wife back in Willcox was pining away for him, and would even file for divorce if he didn't return to Arizona. If

Alvord had a tender streak in him at all it was for his wife, love-outlaw-style but genuine.

Yes, he knew where Chacon was living. He trusted Judge Barnes, and if that gent had a plan that would result in his freedom he was all for it. Chacon was his friend, but the kind of friend who would shoot him through the groin on the slightest provocation. Freedom was better than friendship—and, sure as hell, he would help Captain Mossman bring Agustin Chacon to Solomonsville—for trial and the gallows. And, too, Alvord had a wounded hand. It was festering, so Cap told him that if he didn't get to a doctor quick he would die.

All this led up to the master plan for the capture of Chacon—the matter of Colonel Greene's thoroughbred race horses, the cream of the blue grass, so near the border, so blissfully unattended.

Cap instructed Alvord to get the help of Billy Stiles, wherever he was, and coax Chacon closer to the border, preferably below Naco. And most of all to get his mouth watering for the racehorses, the kind that would bring a fortune in Guadalajara or Mexico City. Then Cap gave the promise—trial and acquittal for both Alvord and Stiles, and a split in all rewards—equal share for the two outlaws and Cap.

Cap returned to Bisbee to await word from Alvord, and it arrived after dark on September 2, 1902. Billy Stiles himself brought the message: Cap and Billy were to ride to Naco, cross the line, and meet with Alvord and Chacon a short distance below. Chacon had his heart and mind full of English thoroughbreds and was delighted to know that Captain Mossman had resigned from the Arizona Rangers and adopted the vocation of a low-down horse-thief. Besides, Alvord told Chacon that Mossman had recently escaped from jail and that he too was a fugitive in Mexico.

Cap and Stiles set out the next morning on the greatest adventure of the Ranger Captain's life. They met Alvord and Chacon in the San Jose mountains below Naco. They greeted each other in Spanish, and if Cap possessed the iron nerve he was noted for he certainly had use for it then. They talked, each man seated in his saddle. Chacon itched to hear more about Colonel Bill Greene's horses. They were the finest mares east of California, Cap made it known, or west of Kentucky. Or for that matter there was nothing to match them in all North America. And the one stallion among them would bring a fortune when the whole herd was driven down to Hermosillo and shipped for sale in Mexico City.

Cap's shining hour was but a night away. All men were heavily armed with revolvers and rifles, and Chacon had a bowie knife sheathed to his belt. They dismounted, unsaddled and staked out the horses for the night. Chacon propped himself against a tree, morose, full of hate, suspicious. And Cap felt sure Stiles and Chacon would kill *him* if the opportunity should arise. But he trusted Alvord. The outlaw was working for a reprieve and reward. And to fill his agreement for help with capture of Chacon he had little more to do.

Cap suggested they get some whiskey and told Billy Stiles to ride into Naco for a bottle. The sun had long dropped behind the Huachuca mountains, but the Sonora moon gave a silver brightness to the robbers' roost. Chacon refused a swig of whiskey, never for a second taking his eyes off Cap. If he nursed a mite of tenderness it was thinking sweetly of Colonel Bill Greene's horses.

At daybreak Burt Alvord surprised everyone by saddling his pony with the intent of riding off from the roost. When Chacon asked him where he was going Alvord gave as an excuse his desire for some drinkable water. But Cap knew they would not see him again, his work with the capture complete. Soon it would be time to ride for the boundary, cut the fence and head for the horse pasture so handy to the border. Chacon had tobacco and cigarette papers, so a smoke would be enjoyed by the three. But while lighting up, with a coal from the fire serving as a match, Chacon's eye was taken off Cap for a second, and in the flash of that second Cap drew his revolver, pulled its aim to Chacon, and called, "Get your hands up, and keep them high."

Chacon complied. The most rabid killer in the frontier West sat helpless before the muzzle of Cap Mossman's gun. And to Stiles he said, "Loose his belt, Billy. Throw his guns and that bowie knife off yonder."

Stiles hesitated. Suddenly he felt a twinge of loyalty for the Mexican he long considered a friend, if Chacon had a friend in all the world. But Cap was ready for any tricks.

He barked, "Do what I say, or I'll kill you as sure as hell!"

So Billy Stiles *did* what Cap ordered, and he even locked a set of handcuffs on Chacon.

Stiles saddled the horses while Cap held Chacon covered with his gun. They helped Chacon onto his horse, the guns were collected and bundled behind Stiles' cantle, and all was readied for the trip north. Stiles put a rope around the neck of Chacon's horse and led the outlaw on his pony. Cap took up the rear, with gun in hand ready to cock should an occasion arise.

Northward, straight north. The border town of Naco was about five miles to the east, which they skirted by moving northwest. No need to alert the Rurales there, for this could easily turn into an international incident. Ahead rose the craggy peak of the Mule mountains, with Bisbee nested in and above Brewery Gulch, only eight miles north of the Mexico line. To the east was spread the Sulphur Springs Valley—horizoned by the mighty mountain island in the sky, the Chiricahuas. At the border fence the mounted threesome were forced to stop, for without cutting the wires they could not enter Arizona. For extra security Cap looped his lariat rope around Chacon's neck, holding the other end while high in the saddle.

While Billy Stiles cut the wires Cap looked to the Mules, and as a gift from the Throne of Heaven caught sight of a smoke plume rising from a canyon—a train, a Southern Pacific train, and it was rolling down from Bisbee to circle the rails and ties that would follow the Rio San Pedro north to Benson, there to junction with the Southern Pacific main line east of Tucson. And soon the train would almost run over Cap and his companion bad men. Now, if Cap could only reach the track soon enough and signal the blessing to a stop.

"All right," he shouted to Stiles, "let's lope these horses."

So they caught the train on time, with Cap signaling the engineer, waving his hat center of the rails. The conductor ran down the set of cars all aflutter, fearful of a holdup, relieved that the express car carried no coin or treasure in the safe. Cap pulled Chacon down from his saddle. The conductor, who recognized the Arizona Ranger captain, was full of cooperation.

"Get the guns and horses into Bisbee, Billy," Cap said to Stiles, "and keep your silly mouth shut. You've done your duty and Judge Barnes will make you a free man."

The drummers seated in the smoking car gaped with amazement, for two more passengers boarded the train and walked down the aisle. One was a tall man with the badge of a United States deputy marshal pinned to his shirt, the other a huge bearded Mexican glaring like a trapped leopard. The latter was handcuffed, and the rope around his neck was held by the man with the badge who also gripped a cocked single-action Bisley Colt's revolver.

By sublime luck the Sheriff of Graham county was on the platform when the train pulled into Benson. When Cap was relieved of his prisoner he returned to Bisbee and prepared to leave Arizona forever. His mind was full of Thatcher & Bloom, and he boarded another train to make Trinidad, Colorado, his destination.

What became of Burt Alvord and Billy Stiles? Well, Burt Alvord just rode into Bisbee, to look up Judges Barnes. He got his share of the reward money, stood trial, and was acquitted. He dug up the loot out by Willcox Dry Lake, more wealth than a man would need for the rest of his life—earned by the holdup of a train near Cochise Junction. He picked up his loving wife, headed for the coast and boarded a ship for Panama, where he died a few years later. And Billy Stiles, rascal that he was, got in trouble again in Cochise County. The sheriff tracked him to Casa Grande, arrested and handcuffed him and was ready to load him on a night stagecoach for Tombstone. But he felt sorry for his prisoner, took him to a saloon and bought him some whiskey, even freed him of his handcuffs. While they sipped their refreshment Billy Stiles tripped the sheriff and pushed him to the floor, made a fast exit of a rear door and escaped into the greasewood—and he was never seen or heard of again.

So the years ahead spelled New Mexico for Cap, that big wide scope of territory where he first worked for cowboy wages, the point of origin of his greatness, to adventure the most valiant men could envy. In 1916 Mahlon Thatcher and Frank Bloom gave him a job, as general manager of their mighty Diamond A empire. And then, on another lucky day, while living as a family man in Roswell, he invested for himself in the huge Turkey Track out by Bullalo Valley.

Cap was nowhere around back in 1902 when the court in Solomonsville for the second time sentenced Chacon to be hanged by the neck, when the bearded desperado said, "I am a man, not afraid to die." . . . Nor was Cap on the scaffold when on November 23rd following Chacon dropped to his death after bidding the sheriff, "Adios, amigo."

And where was Cap, for heaven's sake?

Why, in New York City, in Colonel Bill Greene's suite in the Waldorf Astoria, after years of rugged and ridiculous flirting with death in the Bloody Basin, on the Hashknife, along the border south of the Mule mountains and Brewery Gulch. For Colonel Bill Greene, the copper magnate, sportsman and cattleman, was grateful along with all Arizona to Cap for bringing Chacon across the line to justice. And Cap was much obliged to his multimillionaire friend for the use of his thoroughbred mares and stallion in bringing the capture about.

So that's how come we saw Cap of the snow-white hair walking down to the corner of Second and Main in Roswell, from his office upstairs of the First National Bank, to talk cowboy talk with the cattlemen congregated there. To Gus Chandler or his brother Elv, to Lee Corn or Tobe Foster, to Cort Marley or to Jess Corn, old Jess in from his ranch on the Macho at Eden Valley. To the sheepmen of the Hondo Hills, like Jud McKnight or Lloyd Treat. Or maybe Sam Butler was in town that day, so Cap would ask him how the Rafter S mules were getting along out around Crow Flat.

The last years of Cap's life were enjoyed in his home in Roswell with devoted wife, amid the extensive green of watered lawns and spreading shade trees, where he played host to his countless friends, recalling his adventures in stories he alone was left to tell. Even though severe arthritis had taken his once-strong limbs and robust frame, crippled the hand that a half-century before carried the sharpest, most precise pistol-arm in the West, he lived the greatness of the land with his collection of paintings and Western art, Russells and Remingtons among them. He died in 1956 at the age of eighty-nine.

Sometimes he would eat dinner (noon meal) with us at Diamond A headquarters, out from Roswell to look around and talk business with Ed Bloom, Uncle Frank's nephew, the manager there. On one visit, I remember, in the fall of 1926, I suffered from a nasty toothache and needed the attention of Dr. Pearson, the dentist upstairs along Roswell's Main Street. Cap offered to give me a ride into town.

As the car took the bumps along the rutty road we talked of things that interested him, and on learning that I came from Scotland he told me of his friendship with the many Scottish cattlemen he knew, friends then and in the century past—men such as John Clay of the Swan Cattle Company in Wyoming and Murdo Mackenzie of the great and mighty Matadors. And I told him of how I loved New Mexico, and the ranch life, and the people of substance I had gotten to know. And then I did something rash.

I admitted that my greatest ambition in life was to become a writer and give to the world in print the wonderful West that had become my home, that would be my home for all the years of my life. I waited for a rebuff, but it didn't come. He just chewed on his stogie for a minute or two. The cattlemen and cowboys of the West, I knew too well, had little use for such a fragile thing as literature.

"Go to it, boy," he said, wrangling the stogie, "and do your damnedest."

He drove on, and the silence of the confessional overtook the car's interior. Then he gave a nod of his frosty head backwards toward the Diamond A. "But don't let them fellers back in the bunkhouse know you want to be a writer. Because if you do you'll lose their respect, sure as hell." It was sage advice, the best in the West. So I never confessed my unwholesome intention and thereby kept their respect.

Eleven
The Sugarloaf Mountains

The Peloncillo mountains belong to the extreme southwest corner of New Mexico, sharing with Arizona a serpentine course down the state line southward from below Clifton, to end in a mingling with the Guadalupe range at the New Mexico-Sonora border; where, once across the boundary they become the Sierra de las Espuelas, the northernmost peaks of Mexico's mighty Sierra Madre Occidental.

Sometimes along the way the Peloncillos are in New Mexico, the state line always in their midst. At other places they range in Arizona. Their total distance from north to south approximates 135 miles, one of the longest mountain chains in the Southwest, a region noted for great distances, and for a history brimful with valor and empirebuilding, violence and outlawry, drama, pathos and humor.

Peloncillo (Spanish for *sugarloaf*) is probably the most appropriate name ever applied to a jagged, pinnacled wall of desert rock. Its colors change as the sun journeys up and over the Animas and Hatchet ranges at the east horizon, to fall behind Arizona's magnificent Chiricahua and Dos Cabezas at the set of twilight. Buff is the predominating daytime color of the barren and forbidding Peloncillos. There are isolated spots favorable to juniper and piñon, even living springs of water, occasional patches of pine, but the gravelly soil between rocky upheavals is more harmonious to mesquite and catclaw, cactus and prickly pear, sundry varieties of yucca and other thorny vegetables. Viewed from the valleys below, the Peloncillos appear as the product of some giant Mexican confectioner doing tricks with cones and needles, escarpments and sheer cliffs, dark caves and narrow canyons in an effort to create a sugarloaf wonderland.

The wide sweep of three desert valleys flank the Peloncillos at the west—the Whitlock Valley at the north, just below the Gila River and entirely in Arizona. Farthest south down the range is the San Bernardino at the southeast corner of our neighbor state. But center and for the greatest distance is the San Simon Valley, the wide horizons of its greasewood flats shared by both sovereigns by grace of the state line.

First known as the Sauz Valley (Spanish for *willow*) truly civilized living stayed away from this region until 1883, when J. H. Parramore and Clabe Merchant, cattlemen of Abilene, Texas, drove in some 12,000 head of stock and set up headquarters of the San Simon Cattle Company at the Cienega (Spanish for *marshland*) north of the present village of Rodeo and some twenty miles south of San Simon Siding on the Southern Pacific Railroad. The rails from El Paso connected with California points, having been laid across the valley three years before. Even then, things tender and loving were conspicuously absent. Apaches were hostile and outlaws were everywhere.

One of the most memorable of early Anglo inhabitants was the Reverend J. A. Chenoweth who homesteaded the Cienega long before the cattlemen arrived, and held on to his land in spite of them. Born in Tennessee in 1813, he moved to Texas in 1854, where his religion was said to be full of fire and brimstone and pitchfork-packing devils, which naturally led to some quite noisy sermons. He was a good man with a six-shooter. He sent a note to the outlaw, Black Jack Ketchum, threatening to kill him "sure as hell" if he ever tried to steal a horse from him, and he frightened Cochise and his Apache band with his dancing and "acting crazy." He killed a man at the robbers' roost of Galeyville, high in the Chiricahuas, and obligingly preached his funeral.

Landmarks parade down the range from north to south, places and formations with names to suit the terrain—peaks and canyons, towns at the base of either slope, alive or "gone ghost," some bearing the names of "long gone" characters dear to the recollections of the older inhabitants up and down the adjacent valleys. But the Peloncillos are peculiarly shy of the human presence. The range is in the view of Duncan and San Simon, both in Arizona, and even in the eastside haze of Douglas. On the New Mexico side they may be seen from Lordsburg, Virden, Cotton City and Animas. Rodeo (pronounced *Ro*-dee-oh) lies hard against them in the San Simon (pronounced San See-mohn) Valley.

The village of Rodeo got its start with the building of the El Paso & Southwestern railroad in 1902, the line extending up the valley from Douglas to Antelope Pass in the Peloncillos, from whence it took a course east for El Paso. This became the "Golden State Route" of the joint Rock Island-El Paso & Southwestern Southern Pacific, once the way of the luxurious *Golden State Limited*. The route has been discontinued and the rails and crossties hauled away.

Rodeo gets its name as a long-ago railroad shipping point for livestock, for the many cattle operations once in the area—*rodeo*, being the Spanish for "roundup." Its chief claim to fame is dated from 1915, when Arizona went alcoholically dry and New Mexico remained wet. Its site only a mile from the state line on the road to Douglas, blessed it as the point of export of illegal booze into abstaining territory. Seventeen wholesale liquor establishments went into business, thirty-five saloons prospered. A notable train called "The Drummers' Special" changed its name to "The Drunkards' Special"—hauling in "cotton spitting" pilgrims to the pint-sized depot, then loading saturated, satisfied westbound revelers for the journey out. The three hotels overflowed continuously, prospective guests camped on the street while waiting accommodations. Ragtime bands blasted away day and night, the hellish din resounding up Owl and Mauser canyons to the summits adjacent to the Maloney Ranch. The Turkey Trot was the dance in fashion and the girls at the Goat Ranch did a land-office business. Threlkeld's Hotel fed the Arizonans sumptuously—until 1918, when the nation sank into the gloom of prohibition and Rodeo's three-year whiskey boom suddenly "passed out."

Tall tales laced with humor are rampant up and down the Peloncillos. Somehow they change as time proceeds. Some have lived on since before the turn of the century. One concerns a man of the San Simon Valley who in 1908, after an act of banditry, buried his loot "somewhere south of Rodeo"—was caught, tried and sentenced to a long term of hard labor at the Territorial Prison at Yuma. The judge specified Yuma, nowhere else. In 1909 the Arizona penitentiary was transferred to Florence and the Yuma establishment ceased to exist. As it was beyond the law to confine a prisoner in a nonexistent jail the outlaw of the San Simon was set free, dug up his treasure and lived prosperously ever after.

Another story has a certain Jack Maloney riding down from Paradise in the Chiricahuas in his Model T Ford, top down and open to the skies. He met a coiled rattlesnake at the roadside, which struck at his wheel, tangled in the spokes, and was hoisted high in the air. The reptile descended, only to land on the seat beside Maloney. The driver jumped, leaving the vehicle to continue down the road to Rodeo alone with its venomous hitchhiker.

Another tells of a cattle roundup near Rodeo. The chuck wagon was camped a short distance from the railroad tracks, the cook busy at his fire and potrack, but for some reason the cowboys were just idling away their time, hunkered down here and there or sprawling out on their canvas beds. Someone suggested that if they had a couple decks of cards they could at least enjoy a game of poker or pitch.

Just then, it is told, an El Paso & Southwestern passenger train (perhaps the Drunkards' Special) was rattling down Antelope Pass in the Peloncillos, westbound, just a few miles to the northeast. With intent to break the monotony the ever-legendary Jack Maloney, together with the Chenoweth boys, stood themselves between the rails and faced the oncoming train.

They waved frantically and the engineer responded. At the time it was customary for cowboys to pack guns. As the group held the engineer and fireman frozen with hands hoisted, one boarded the train and purchased two decks of cards from the "butcher boy" in the smoking car. The same story, however, is told about a Southern Pacific train near Benson, and another located somewhat to the north when a dozen Hashknife cowboys and a Santa Fe train gave Holbrook the honors. Folktales concerning cowboys come in wide latitudes.

An unbridled sense of humor is God's gift to people who live with the thorny, squint-eyed, dusty, dry-throat life-style of the desert. But the history of it all is loaded with tragedy, too. Valleys stretch westward from the dinosaur backbone of the Peloncillos for three hundred miles—the San Simon, the Sulphur Springs, San Bernardino, San Pedro, Santa Cruz, and onward across the Lower Sonoran to the torrid rut called the Colorado. And mountains—besides the Chiricahuas are the Huachucas, the Whetstones, the Santa Catalinas and a hundred other earth-bare peaks as seen from the desert floor, but all alive with nature's moving things, the banquet-spread of a botanist's paradise. With history—wild and woolly and full of wonders. Tales of valor, and the sacrifice that builds an Empire.

Tombstone is famed for its wild west story, so is Cochise Stronghold in the high Dragoons—and the Superstitions and almost every square mile of what is called the Lower Sonoran. But what about the great lonesome stretch of New Mexico that piles and dips itself eastward over mountain range and fertile or arid valley, along the Chihuahua border to the Paso del Norte and beyond?

There are towns, of course, along highways and railroads—Lordsburg, Deming, Las Cruces, Alamogordo, Carlsbad, Hobbs, all polished and aglitter with altitudes in the four thousand foot range or below, the benevolent sun a ticket to their fame and fortune. But what about the alkali flats, and the mountains of the Playas that heave and quiver in the summertime heat, the sinks between where only the hardiest of desert growth may survive, the bone-dry grit and gravel of it all under a sky the color of steel?

In the extreme southwest corner of the state is Cloverdale, where the Peloncillo mountains merge with the Guadalupes to meet Sonora south of Black Peak and Outlaw Mountain. But please, don't picture Cloverdale as a place of three-leaved legumes that carpet a rich moist soil, or a dale fed by refreshing springs. It is not that sort of place at all. It was once a Victorio Cattle Company line camp, today one of the loneliest spots in America.

Peloncillo country is "Clanton Country," and the Clanton boys were the most notorious family of outlaws ever to "romanticize" in their crude way New Mexico, Arizona, Chihuahua, and Sonora. They were contemporary with Curly Bill Brocius, John Ringo, Johnny-Behind-the-Deuce, the Earp confederacy, the Apache Kid, and sundry others familiar with the Sugarloaf Mountains. Not to exclude Geronimo and Mangus Coloradas. Though the latter two were not outlaws but patriots.

Further down the range, south of Woodchoppers Spring and north of Clanton Draw, is Skeleton Canyon—a veritable "Hell's Kitchen" of the early day, now the home of peaceful, law abiding cattleman Benny Snoor and his family. They occupy the old Ross Sloan ranch house which stands, as does the Miller home in Post Office Canyon, to mark the entrance to a long-defunct pack-horse trail for smugglers operating into and from Mexico.

Two wild encounters took place near the ranch house, involving outlaws and smugglers, the first almost at the front door. It was a gun battle fierce enough to shame a modern Hollywood horse-and-havoc flick, which left sundry cadavers for wolves and coyotes and their hearty appetites—after the loot was hauled to Galeyville. The second battle, more of a massacre, occurred in 1882 when Curly Bill Brocius and his gang of ruffians ambushed a long pack-mule train of contraband on the Arizona-New Mexico territorial line, the Mexicans trekking across the Peloncillos bound for Chihuahua, about a mile east of the Ross Sloan domicile. The Mexicans had been raiding and looting in Arizona. Fifteen smugglers were killed, their bodies left in the sunshine to be torn apart by the ravenous predators. Bones and skulls were scattered over a wide area, in later years to be picked up as souvenirs by cowboys, hunters and prospectors, the skulls now serving as conversation pieces and bits of skeleton making excellent living room ashtrays—hence the name of the canyon.

It was in Skeleton Canyon, even closer to the present-day Snoor home, that a greater event happened to grace the chronicles of American history. Here, on September 5, 1886, the Apache leader Geronimo capitulated to Lieutenant Charles Gatewood of the United States Army, who met the Indian alone and unarmed. He accepted the surrender and thus ended five years of Apache warfare, raiding and looting of white settlements in New Mexico and Arizona. A monument marks the spot, a short mile and a quarter west of the New Mexico boundary.

Up the state line from Steins Pass and the village of Steins, completely in New Mexico, Steins Peak rises to a summit of 5,867 feet, a thousand feet above the Braidfoot Ranch at its base. Also in its shadow are the ruins of the old E. Garrison Relay station, once an important horse-change stop on the Butterfield stagecoach trail that was in business from 1857 to 1861.

Steins Peak, an insignificant blister when compared with the bulk and altitude of other New Mexico mountains, is mighty with a history of Wild West adventure and a challenge to the early day empire builders. Here at the stagecoach station a squad of cavalrymen were handy to accompany the coaches west through Doubtful Canyon, a narrow rocky chasm popular with the Apache for ambush and massacre of hated white intruders. Hence the name—East Garrison—but in spite of the soldiers' presence the assaults continued.

At the west base of the peak, a quarter mile into Arizona, is the gravestone of John James Giddings, in life the traffic manager of the Butterfield Texas division, who met his end with other company officials in April, 1861, when their coach overturned and the Apaches engaged in the slaughter. Giddings was held for special treatment—torture, mutilation and eventual death. Later Cochise, while describing the horror at Janos in Chihuahua, made comment that Giddings "died like a sick woman." The gravestone was erected by Giddings's daughter in 1925 when she visited the spot. To reach the peak, the relay station and the gravestone today, one enters the canyon by a dirt road north off Interstate Highway 10 a mile or so east of San Simon, Arizona.

Tragedy, violence, a man's greed or arrogance rising in defiance of another man's trust, the Apache war cry and crack of the six-shooter, exercise of the hang rope and acts of inhumanity that stagger the imagination, common to the Lower Sonoran as elsewhere in the territorial West, were all part of the business of taming a frontier—gone forever to make fascinating the pages of history. The deathless story of the "good guys and the bad guys" is meat for youngest America watching the television screen. Today the Sugarloaf Mountains and the few towns adjacent enjoy a legacy of peaceful living, freedom from the crime menace so prevalent elsewhere in America, made possible by the stalwart no-nonsense nature of its people.

The Guadalupe Canyon area, close to where the Peloncillos give way to the mountains of Sonora, is where the lover of wild magnificence may feast for days—easily reached by the Geronimo Trail that spans the range, starting at bustling Douglas, eastward out of Arizona, or from forlorn Cloverdale on the New Mexico side of the line.

Here is a section of the Coronado National Forest that contains within its boundaries almost every variety of desert fauna and flora common to the Lower Sonoran, except perhaps the vegetable species found in the lowest altitudes of Arizona and Sonora, such as the saguaro and organpipe cactus. Undisturbed are creosote bush, opuntia, mesquite, yucca, century plant, snakeweed, and chaparral. At the upper levels thrive oak and mountain laurel, madrona and manzanita, piñon and barberry, juniper and pine.

Wildlife ranges in profusion, sheltering in the canyons and above the limestone cliffs—whitetail deer, wild turkeys, coyotes, mountain lions, an abundance of smaller furred creatures including the coati-mundi. Stockmen further up the Peloncillos complain about intruding border wolves whose habitat is Mexico and have no respect for international boundaries. Birdwatchers find paradise in Guadalupe Canyon, where hummingbirds flutter in galore. Javalinas (wild hogs) grunt and squeal on the hillsides above the Trail. Reptiles are in extra abundance, including the deadly Sonoran coral snake and the Gila Monster. Rattlesnakes—diamondbacks, blacktails; and a stray very rare ridge-nosed rattlesnake native to the nearby Animas mountains, was recently put on the federal list of endangered wildlife species.

As the Peloncillo Mountains are scenically dramatic, unique are the place names up and down the jagged backbone. Besides Skeleton and Post Office canyons, there is Clanton Draw that gives way to the Geronimo Trail—both names perpetuating frontier history. There is Dutchman Canyon and Bunk Robinson Peak, Big and Little Skull canyons. Lion Creek and Maverick Spring, Cowboy Flats.

The guns of the past are done with, and peace and serenity rule the Sugarloaf Mountains. The air is clean, and the sunshine unhindered except for scarce occasions when the blessed, prayed-for rains fall on the ever-thirsty land. And people, the old-timey settlers who had minds and opinions vastly different from those who are finding their way in—newcomers to develop and build the future of it all—for better or for worse. In the early years of the present century, when the frontier was passing to make way for a frailer, more artificial method of life, the poet Badger Clark rode as a cowboy in the Lower Sonoran, and summarized the landscapes and people in verse called "The Border," one of many poems in his book *Sun and Saddle Leather*.

His three-page song gives tribute to the land, its prehistories and histories, Coronado, Kino, the first battlers of the wild; the outlaws, the miners, the drovers, the grazers, the hucksters, the merchants, the preachers, the good and bad of them all. But more delicately he pictures the earth and its apparel, the gleaming yucca, the cactus and the myriad wild flowers, its moods in the dazzling heat and swirling dust, the song of the mockingbird and whirr of the rattler, the coyote call. He praises the serenity, the thousand freedoms there for the taking, the elbow room, the brightness:

> Vast peace, the clear sky's earthy double,
> Witch cauldron forever abubble,
> Home of mystery, splendor and trouble,
> And a people with sun in their veins.

Twelve
The Ghost Girl of the Mimbres

Of all the ghosts that have ever haunted New Mexico, there was none like the Ghost Girl of the Mimbres.

New Mexico has its familiar ghosts, of course, La Llorona, the weeping woman, all shrouded in black. The ghost that carries his severed head under his arm. Tapping ghosts, moaning ghosts, thumping ghosts. Things that go bump in the night. Standard ghosts all, none with qualities that set one spirit apart from another.

None, for example, like the Ghost Girl of the Mimbres—graceful horsewoman, meticulously garbed and with physical features as beautiful as ever seen on any female.

And stranger still, her haunting ground was—or *is*?—that southerly section of New Mexico lying between the Burro mountains on the west and the Mimbres Range on the east—the greasewood flats under the cleanest, brightest sun in America. No place for a ghost—unless it be the kind she was, capable of stirring romantic curiosity and tender thoughts in the roughest of men.

Her story first apparently came to light in October 1906 in an article in the Chicago *Tribune*, quoted a few days later in the Albuquerque *Evening Citizen* and discovered and quoted by Howard Bryan in the Albuquerque *Tribune* in 1961.

The apparition was described as an extraordinarily beautiful girl, probably in her twenties, riding a fleet bay horse and garbed in a riding habit fashionable at the time—with her long hair tastefully groomed under a widebrimmed felt hat. Her polished leather boots and silver spurs shone in the intense Mimbres sun. She was tall, slender and graceful in the saddle. Some reports noted her "Spanish features."

On a morning in May 1906, Pete Bianca, a cowboy, was riding a pasture near the Crossing of the Mimbres. This was once an important watering point on the old Butterfield stage line north of what is now Deming. The river here, after descending from its source in the Black Range, presents itself as a small stream before going underground and continuing down across the Mexican border to come to light as the Laguna de Guzman in Chihuahua, about thirty miles south of Columbus.

Faithful to duty, Pete Bianca had his mind on cows, not girls, as he trotted his pony down a trail. Suddenly he reined his mount to a stop. His sun-squinted eyesight had caught a glimpse of a young woman trotting her horse ahead of him toward the Mimbres Crossing. Her dress was unfamiliar, more suited to the green fields of the Eastern states than the raw, gravelly greasewood desert. Women of the district in those days were homemakers for their ranchmen husbands and fathers, champions of the cookstove. They left horseback work to the menfolks. They wore long dresses and aprons and sunbonnets.

Neither Pete Bianca nor any of the horsemen who later met up with the girl described her as riding sidesaddle, the favored riding style for women in those days. But all were emphatic about the horse's being a fleet thoroughbred—not the wiry little Spanish cowpony of the border country. Here was a stranger come to the Mimbres and Pete Bianca was curious. He spurred his pony into a lope, his intent to catch up with her. He stopped when he saw her reach the Crossing. She dismounted, removed her hat and bent to give her horse and herself a drink from the stream. Pete watched and gulped with amazement, for she was very beautiful. Then, with almost supernatural grace, she mounted and took a trail leading to Dan Taylor's ranch. She rode at a trot, while the cowboy followed at a distance.

The girl had disappeared among the bushes by the time Pete rode up to the ranch. Taylor was in the saddle shed when Pete called "Howdy." The girl wasn't around anywhere. Pete suspected he would find her either in the corral with her horse or wherever Dan happened to be. Dan, a bachelor, came from the shed holding a latigo and Pete asked about the girl. Dan looked puzzled as he told Pete he had nothing as lovely as that stocked on his ranch. In fact, the nearest woman was miles away and not likely to be out on horseback.

"I'll show you her tracks," Pete said. "I followed them in from out yonder."

Dan saddled up and the two loped out to the road. No hooftracks anywhere. But a little further on they came to prints of a shod horse.

"That ain't our kind of pony," Dan said in puzzlement.

"I saw the horse," Pete said.

They looked at the tracks—plain as daylight—where they led toward the Taylor ranch and then just stopped, of a sudden, as if horse and rider had faded off the Mimbres earth.

"Hell, Pete," Dan Taylor said. "You must have seen a ghost."

Ed Tuttle ran a bunch of cows on his ranch close by the copper-pit sprawl of Santa Rita. One day in early summer he rode at a fast trot along the trail to town, thinking perhaps of something pleasant—like cows. Of a sudden he saw what appeared to be a woman on horseback ahead, just dawdling along at a walk as though she hadn't much to do. He raised his hat as he passed her, and kept on going. But he did notice her attire—tan riding outfit, felt hat, and the brightness of her boots, the shine of her silver spurs—and her horse, one built and gaited like none other thereabouts. A horse truly beautiful, but no more so than his rider. That girl, thought Ed Tuttle, was the prettiest he'd ever seen anywhere.

On Santa Rita's main street he met up with some bowlegged gents he knew, cattlemen and cowboys, all in town on either business or a binge. Maybe both. He asked who the beautiful lady was, and when did she arrive to pretty up Santa Rita.

Everybody up and down the street said as how they knew of no girl like that, and especially no horse of that kind.

Ed Tuttle shook his head, perplexed.

To satisfy the curiosity growing in him, Ed rode around the country, asked if anybody knew of the girl on horseback, quizzed folks around Deming and Silver City, Hudson Hot Springs, Fort Bayard, maybe Lordsburg. But not a soul knew about her. Some, in fact, began to figure Ed had had one too many that day and was seeing things.

A short while later a corporal at Fort Bayard gave Ed Tuttle the satisfaction he longed for.

"I was riding along the road near Georgetown—came upon a woman just sitting in the saddle of her bay horse, not moving. I raised my hat politely. Thought maybe she was an officer's wife. And all she did was spur her horse and wheel him around—to lope off and disappear right in the middle of the road."

The corporal described the lady. Spanish, sort of. Olive skin and brown hair pinned up neatly under a broad-brimmed felt hat. Her face as chiseled and refined as any soldier could see. Slender in her tan riding dress, and the way she handled the horse was grace itself. She had the dignity of a general's wife, but much better looking.

"That's her," said Ed Tuttle.

The July night was bright as moonlight can make it when Bert Cooper rode home from a day in Silver City—just a cowboy on the town.

He came to a rise on the trail, as he later told a group of listeners, "and I saw her just ahead of me, sitting in her saddle, taking it easy. The moonlight lit her up and I high-loped my pony, and we took out after her."

But alas for poor Bert. The girl wheeled her horse and sashayed on ahead of him.

"She went out of sight all of a sudden, and all I could hear was the clatter of the horse hoofs. Beats me how she did it because that pony of mine can outrun anything alive."

"Maybe she wasn't alive," a cowboy said.

Strange things were happening along the Mimbres that summer, because the Ghost Girl was sighted by sane folks all over the district.

The girl got more familiar as the hot months moved along. A gent named Navajo Andrews passed her in broad daylight on a trail against the west slope of the Florida Mountains south of Deming. He didn't try to "mess with her"—he just let her be. She waved to him as he rode on, then she turned and took off at a lope toward the Crazy S Ranch.

A short time later Fletch Burke was riding after some calves, minding his own business, when she rode up right beside him, the prettiest thing he had ever seen, up on a horse like none other in New Mexico. Fletch greeted her as a gentleman should, raising his hat. She smiled at him with the sweetest smile, then reined away without a word. The hoofs made clatter as she went into nothing.

Fletch could have reached out and touched her when she came up close. But he didn't. He was too polite.

Do you believe in ghosts? At first Pete Bianca didn't, then he did. Likewise Dan Taylor, and Ed Tuttle, and Bert Cooper, and lots of folks around the Mimbres. When cowboys met up with the pretty girl on the bay horse they'd brag on her, say how she was a ghost worth knowing, even though the acquaintance was silent and lasted only a few minutes.

But *was* she a ghost? Some argued that she couldn't be, for real ghosts suddenly appear, make themselves seen or heard, maybe deliver a message, then disappear leaving no trace. This one didn't speak, but she had waved a "Howdy" to Navajo Andrews. Her horse made sound with the clatter of his hoofs. Again, ghost horses might make clatter, but they just don't leave tracks—this one *did*.

Or maybe she was not a ghost, but a dream—a dream projected from the intense mind of a distant girl. A girl in Savannah . . . or Sussex . . . or Seville. A girl who, like New Mexico's fabled Blue Lady, was willing herself to be somewhere else, far from a forced marriage, a fevered sickbed, the sorrow of a lost love. A girl who dreamed of sandy gravel deserts, creosote brush, pinnacled mountains heaving in the noonday sun.

Then, when the summer of 1906 gave way to autumn, the Ghost Girl of the Mimbres made her farewell appearance, and those privileged to witness the event were three bowlegged riding men from the Flying Y Ranch, up there north of Deming. They were Sam Teener, Manuelo Yeros and Mont Steen. They were earning their wages, riding after cattle, not girls on horseback. The ground they traveled was flat with greasewood and ahead was that landmark extraordinary, the desert wonder called The City of Rocks. A Stonehenge-type rock formation, it gets its name from the illusion of a metropolitan skyline when seen from a distance.

So let's have Sam Teener tell the story of that September day.

"Well, me and Mont Steen and Manuelo Yeros was out there near the warm springs and we saw her aset on her horse, looking at the City of Rocks. She just gazed at it, like it was hers, like she aimed to do something with it. Old Mont and me and Manuelos reined up our ponies. We were bug-eyed. It was the Ghost Girl, all right. And she looked like she was going somewhere, because she had her hat pulled back on its chin-strap to let the sun shine on her pretty brown hair. She sat in the saddle, primping up, and she held something by her lips, a hairpin, like we see the ladies do front of a mirror—and all the while she and her horse looked toward The City. Take it from me, she was the most beautiful woman I ever saw. I couldn't reckon what she was doing along the Mimbres.

"Old Mont quizzed me about what we should do. I said, 'Let's go git her.' I raised my hat and called, 'Miss, good morning.' She didn't pay me a lick of mind. So me and Mont spurred our ponies into a lope. We got about fifty yards from her when she smiled at us, touched her horse with her spurs and was off across the flat.

"Mont and me, we tried to head her off. But she was too quick. Manuelo wasn't any good. He knew she was a ghost, and kept crossing himself. Me and Mont ran our horses like they'd never run before. She got to where the rocks stood high off the ground, and just before she got behind the biggest of them, we saw the last of her."

That's how Sam Teener told it, and he swore to the end that he didn't believe in ghosts. "Ghosts don't leave no souvenirs," he claimed.

The three men combed The City of Rocks, but not a sign of the Ghost Girl could they find. The hoofprints ended behind the rock where she was last seen. The cowboys walked their horses back to the spot where they first saw her, where she sat on her horse primping up pretty. There the prints showed plain as daylight.

Then, Sam Teener's sharp eye caught something else, something glittering on the ground. He dismounted, bent to pick it up.

It was a hairpin.

Thirteen
The Last Narrow Shave

I can't remember for certain what we had for supper that night, but I'm pretty sure it consisted of bacon in a skillet, pinto beans with salt pork in a pot, fried potatoes in a heavy dutch oven resting to the side in a bed of oak-coals—and Arbuckle's coffee as black as coffee can be brewed. There were side dishes of rice and raisins, stewed prunes or dried peaches, and several cans of tomatoes dumped into a bucket—and molasses lick, lots of lick.

Maybe beef steaks, if we'd butchered a yearling, cut from the carcass and wrapped in Fish Brand saddle slickers. We loaned the slickers to the cook for the purpose. It hadn't rained, nor was it likely.

It's hard to remember after more than half-a-century, but that was a cowboy supper and we were out by the Lutz Well on the Patos Draw, eating pretty at the chuck wagon. Bob Paterson was the wagon cook. It was July, and we'd put the Bridle Bit brand on rounded-up calves all day long—combing the North Pasture and driving little bunches down to the gathered herd at the Lutz corrals; heeling little calves out from next to their mothers and dragging them by saddle-horn and lariat rope to the branding fire where the flankers would hold them to the ground, while the iron-man stunk up the air with burning hair and hide, while the roper played with his loop and fixed to catch another calf by the heels.

We'd held the herd while the straymen from neighbor ranches rode in on their cutting ponies, to haze out any strays from their own outfits that had come through the fences and joined the Bridle Bit stock. All that, and a lot of hard riding.

And at day's end—Lord, we were tired!

Next day we would move the camp to the Corn Well a dozen miles to the south, where we'd perform the whole dusty, stinking, sweaty, saddle-weary Act Two of the roundup over again—but right then it was supper time after turning our ponies loose in the remuda. We sat on the ground or atop our rolled-up beds in their canvas tarps, just eating as daintily as we could out of our tin plates. All the chuck the cook gave us. Lon and Bug, sons of the Old Boss himself, had already driven off home to Headquarters for the night. They went in the Tin Lizzie Ford pickup truck—one that needed jacking up the hind wheel to get it started. We were glad to be left alone so we could cuss both boys out in private and talk about their sundry misbehavior. The Ford must have been a 1922 model, and here it was 1929. Like the Big Boss, who hadn't come out to the roundup that day, it was showing age, although pickups lasted longer in those days than they do now.

The day had been hot, and now we were thankful the sun had set. Cool twilight dropped down on our camp and a sweet night's sleep was on hand. We spread out our bedrolls to loll and roll a smoke, some to chew cud and tell frightful lies about all we knew. About men and horses, cattle, and women—but mostly to give ourselves shocking self-praise. It was an evening of a happy year between wars, when plastic and steel, gasoline, and the touch of machine-buttons belonged to some time and space hundreds of miles away, when the Taylor Grazing Act of 1934 was far in the future, the Cowboy Riding Country hadn't quite wiped frontier dust from off its grass and arroyos. When the Long Water Hole on the Carrizo Draw held its green-slick wetness from one rain to another.

Lord, we were a rested and content bunch of bean-eaters!

Until a bay pony trotted into our midst and high in the saddle was the Old Boss, chief-cook-and-bottle-washer of the whole Bridle Bit ranch, and it looked like he'd come to spend the night.

We were flabbergasted, our privacy had gone with the campfire smoke!

"Howdy, boys, howdy," he said off his high saddle perch.

The greeting was friendly, all right, but we all hoped the voice wasn't real, that we'd gone to sleep and were dreaming off a bad dream.

But it *was* real, for we heard the jingle of spurs and creak of saddle-leather and flap of chap-wings and a human grunt as the aged rider dismounted from his pony. In silence we eyed him with hostile looks and the wagon cook ducked his head in shame as he fixed to clean up after supper. With expert aim the old rider let fly a squirt of amber, to land it far out on the grama grass. Then he said to the cook, "Cook, you needn't put the lids on them pots yet, 'cause I've come out here from Headquarters. I'm mighty hungry, cook. I'm rarin' to eat. If I'd stayed home I'd have eaten my woman. I'm a cannibal at heart, cook. Son, I'm a South Sea Islander. Don't you know my nationality?"

The cook got ready to feed him supper, but the balance of us blushed as we kept respectfully silent.

He unhooked the latigo and let the cinch drop. He pulled the saddle from off his mount, and by such action we knew he intended to spend the night. We puffed on our cigarettes, said nothing, and we sorely itched with aggravation. He'd come out to camp before, pleaded for our hospitality, which meant one of us would be sharing our bed with him—and every man of us was getting sick of it.

He pulled off the bridle. His pony, a bay pacer, trotted off to join the horse herd. That pony knew what he was doing, all right, for he'd done cow-work and grazed with horse herds all his equine life. Measured in horse-years his was almost as long as that of the Old Boss. We didn't like his brazen intrusion on our private session, even if our talk didn't amount to a fiddler's damn. Nobody in that chuck-wagon bunch knew exactly how old the Old Boss was, nor did they care. But I knew for a fact he was seventy-nine.

One of his boys, the younger, told me his dad's history on a day when we were sitting next to the ranch-house fireplace. He was born in a tent where Pilot Point, Texas sits today. So that made him seventy-nine, like I said. There was never a day that wasn't concerned with the cattle range, although one of his sons got to be a state senator up in Wyoming, which didn't last long because he loved cows better than politics. The family name was a prominent one in Texas and had much to do with the founding of Abilene, a city in that Lone Star state.

The Old Boss looked like he'd lived a long time. He was lank of frame and grizzled around the complexion. And as he bent over the potrack to help himself to beans, and fish out a biscuit from the dutch oven, and pour himself a mug of coffee, the mounting on his spurs shone in the firelight, and we knew right then that his eyes shone just as bright—with love, gratitude to God for the life on the range he was privileged to live, way back for so long a time. We said nothing. He kept silent as he hunkered down in the midst of us. We watched him eat his supper. He went to the cook's work-table hind-end of the wagon to pour some molasses lick into his plate. He'd dunk a biscuit in it, a cowboy's favorite dessert. Then he came back to hunker down. He didn't say a damn thing, he just ate. Lord, was he a healthy eater for all his long years!

I remember it wasn't long before that July day, maybe in May, I found him sitting against the low rail inside the corral at Headquarters, alone, and sort of dozing. But he wasn't dozing, he was thinking hard. He came awake when I hunkered down beside him, and he said, "John, I'd sure like to quiz you of a question. Do you believe in God?"

"I sure do," I told him.

"Then where you reckon God wants an old man's bones to be put when it comes time to bury them deep?"

"In the graveyard, I should think," I said.

He said no more, but I knew what he meant. He looked down at the corral-dirt and went to thinking hard.

I knew what he meant by God and his bones, asking me what I thought, because that past winter the younger of his boys got sentimental about his dad. He told me how the Old Boss asked him as to where they'd bury him when he died. And the younger son said, "I reckon it'll be in Artesia, Dad. You've got lots of friends in Artesia."

Then the old man said, "I was hopin' you'd plant me out yonder."

"Where, Dad?"

"Just dig a hole and put me in, out there on the Patos by the Long Water Hole. I like cattle, and I'd like to meet 'em at that green-slimy drink of stock water."

But they didn't bury him next to the water hole in the fall of '29, just a few months after he rode among us at the July roundup camp. He died in a hospital and they buried him in the Artesia cemetery. He had lots of friends there and the funeral procession was nigh a mile long.

And that day, while we both sat together against the corral rail, we had to talk of something else besides God and bones, so I told him I'd just killed the biggest rattlesnake I'd ever seen in the Capitans, by the road that went up to Joe Koprian's place. It had a back full of diamonds and a head as big as a deck of cards. I killed it with rocks just an hour before.

That got him to talking about a time in the Cornudas mountains, where the snakes get bigger than anywhere else in New Mexico, how he was riding out after cattle and the thunder and lightning brought down a deluge of rain something like that which struck Noah. He said he let his pony get wet while he took shelter in a cave, a little cave but big enough to hold a dense population of rattlesnakes. He crawled in slow but he came out fast. A big one struck at his leg, dug a fang in the pants-cuff, not making a scratch. He pulled the fang-stuck snake out as he met the rain, and a lot of venom dripped on his boot heel and spur before he knocked the devil loose.

Then he said to me, "John, believe me, that was *one narrow shave*."

But now July had come and there he was, ridden into the roundup camp, and none of us showed that he was welcome.

He explained it this way, "I'd ridden down to look the stuff over out by the Zamora Well. I just rode around some, not thinkin' how sundown was catchin' up on me. I sure hated to ride that fifteen miles home, so I headed your way, hopin' one of you fellers would half his bed with me for the night."

He spoke that truth about sundown, all right, for he was nearing sundown of his life.

And what had been his gift of God to live through seventy-nine of his daylight years? What all do you reckon?

At the start he'd watched the buffalo roam, and helped his kinfolks build the city of Abilene. He'd dodged tornados as they swept the Blacklands, and he swam through floods come down with the Red River. In 1883 he'd driven twelve thousand cattle west from Abilene with Clabe Merchant and J. H. Parramore to settle the stock in the San Simon Valley on the Arizona-New Mexico territorial boundary, himself a tower of horseman-strength at age thirty-three. And with Clabe being a cousin of sorts, he'd ridden the Merchant ranges on the San Simon Swale east of Carlsbad, in those long-ago days when that city was a Chisum cowcamp.

The lifelong drover that he was, he followed herds up the Chisholm Trail to Abilene, Kansas, and Dodge City, to the railhead points of the Great American Southwest—there to rub shoulders with Bat Masterson, Wyatt Earp, Luke Short, Rowdy Joe Lowe in the Long Branch Saloon, and to sigh with pity when a gunshot ended the sad, sad love-tragedy of Spike Kennedy and Dora Hand. He'd ridden the diverse ranges of Texas, Kansas, Nebraska, Montana—he'd ranched in the Goshen Hole of eastern Wyoming, and watched the Platte start irrigating the breadbasket of America. And, lastly, he'd come out to Lincoln county a few years before to graze his herds on the ranch that spread over the northside flats from the White Oaks Draw to Dry Canyon, from the Macho south to the West Mountain of the Capitans, where sweet water was piped down from Gum Spring amid the pine and balsam.

Aged and saddle-weary, knowing that his sundown was near, all he asked of his long life when the hour should come was eternal rest on Carrizo

158   Chapter Thirteen

Arroyo—where he could "meet 'em at the water hole." And, then, on that night at the roundup camp nearby the Lutz Well, there in all humility he asked one of us at a time for a half-share of a rolled-out bed. That's right, he asked us in all humility.

Lord, were we a heartless bunch!

Not one of us offered a spark of hospitality.

One by one he quizzed us, and every kind of a silly excuse was made. Then, lastly, he said, "John, you've got some tenderness for an old man, more'n that dozen bean-eaters aset there. Won't you loan me half your bed for tonight? You've eaten dinner plenty times in my house."

And to that, I said, "You bet, Mr. Merchant."

The "bunch of bean-eaters" that had hung their heads in dread looked up from their coffee mugs. Each gave a grunt of relief. Now they wouldn't have him tossing around, messing up their slumbers, nudging them to ask how long they reckoned it would be 'til the rise of the sun, wondering why the cook wasn't up to build the fire and fix to make breakfast. As soon as I made my offer they all came alive again, gobbled their talk like turkeys and told him how the work went that day.

The cook's fire was wearing down to coals when I rolled out my bed and fixed the soogans for the night. The old man pulled off his boots and pants and laid them on the grass, topping the little pile with his hat. He didn't take up much space, for age and a life of the most grueling work had worn his frame down to gauntness. He took a chew from his cud-plug and settled down for the night, although his chewing off the quid let me know he wasn't ready for any slumber yet—he just aimed to chew and spit and talk, as the bean-eaters figured he'd do if any of them gave him hospitality.

He lay flat, his head on his rolled-up saddle-blanket pillow, his eyes fixed to look skyward. Tired as hell, I fell off to sleep fast. But soon, what I expected, came to be.

"John," he said, nudging me out of my doze, "you reckon it's midnight yet."

I reached for my turnip-watch, struck a match and said, "Not quite, it's only ten-thirty."

I heard him say, "Hell."

Not quite midnight, now only an hour and a half left of the passing day, soon time to start a new one in the few that remained in the cowboy life of the Old Boss. So short a time left for riding the pacer-pony out to the Lutz Well or just looking over the stuff along the Carrizo. Because a few weeks after that night, like in August, at the Headquarters corral, the younger of his sons told me what happened at the saddle shed the day before. It seems the old man caught his pacer-pony and put on the bridle. He got out the saddle and blanket, and when he had them cinched and set he coiled his lariat and looped it on the string off-side of the saddle-horn. And with that he was fixed to ride out. But he wasn't mounted. All he had to do was put his boot in the stirrup and throw a leg over the cantle. He had the bridle-reins in hand.

"Where you headin' for today, Dad?" quizzed his youngest pride and joy.

"Nowhere partic'lar. Maybe out to Patos Arroyo. Remember what I told you a hundred times, I like to meet 'em at the water-hole."

So he put his booted foot in the stirrup—as he'd done all the years of his life from Texas to Montana, in the Goshen Hole and amid the greasewood of the San Simon Swale. He held the bridle-reins against the pony's mane with his left hand, he gripped the saddle-horn with his right. Then he set to do something he'd done all the sunshine days and starlit nights of his life—to swing into the saddle, to tap old Pacer with a rowel of his spur.

Or, at least, he tried to. But he couldn't. he didn't have the strength anymore.

"Wait a minute, Dad," that younger boy said. "Let me hold old Pacer while you try again."

But words like that put a stab in the old man's heart. He dropped the reins. Then he said, "You needn't do that, son. When a cowpuncher gits so weak he can't mount a horse, then that's the end of his livin' days. Put up my saddle and turn old Pacer out to the pasture." And with that he walked away to the house—and true to his words, he never rode a horse again.

But that night earlier in July, as I shared my bed with him, as I watched him by the moon's light look up to the sky, I wondered about his thoughts, and the opinions he held in his silence. Was the starlight over the Cienega del Macho as bright as that of the Wyoming prairies, and was the silence of the midnight then—silent except for the once in so often bawl of a cow and nicker of a horse, or the sigh of the breeze and the squeak and groan of the Lutz windmill. Were they as full of fuss or contentment as ours in the camp just then?

There were snores all around us, the easy smell of cigarette smoke hinted how one cowpoke was awake. I dozed off to sleep, but soon was nudged into consulting my watch, of telling him how the time was a few minutes past two.

I heard him say, "John, I wonder why them fellers had to be so mean they wouldn't give me a place under the soogans. Don't they know if they should ride up to my house, anytime, I'd feed 'em supper and let 'em stay all night."

Then, finally, to me came a couple hours of blessed sleep.

He nudged me again at the rise of the morning star.

"You see what I see, John," he said. "The cook's up and kindlin' his fire. He'll have coffee fixed in no time at all, and this old settler is ready to he'p him drink it up."

And with such words of joy he was out of my hospitality and ready to meet the chores of the day.

There wouldn't be much to do that day except move the wagon loaded with our bedrolls and the cook's gear over to the Corn Well, to herd the remuda over that way and get ready for the next couple days combing the pasture, branding and cutting out the straymen's strays. So there wasn't much need to hustle, and we ate our breakfast around the potrack with gulps and swigs, to enjoy time to sound off with lies and brags of the most unbecoming proportions.

The Old Boss sat off by himself, just downing his coffee while he crunched bacon and potatoes between his teeth.

I heard one feller say, and was sure the old man heard him too, "I know what I aim to do when I git my check for this here work. I aim to ride chuck-line down to Carrizozo, where I'll make pretty talk with my blonde-headed sweetie there. I aim to stay all night with some old boys along the way, and their womenfolks will fix me supper."

I paid him no mind but gave my glance to the Old Boss. I could see how such words riled him to the core. I saw him put down his plate, then with coffee-mug in hand walk toward us hunkered around the potrack. He took a stand and let off his mouth:

"I heard what you said, boy, and your talk makes me sick like a mule. When you ride chuck-line and ask for a place to stay all night, just you come to my house. My woman will fix you a bed and feed you some steak and eggs with apple pie on the side. We ain't scared to make a bed for a friend in my house."

Lord, how the bean-eaters hung their heads in shame!

"But," he added, "I'm mighty grateful to you all fellers for not givin' me a lick of your hospitality. You saved me from disaster—just by the wideness of *one narrow shave.*"

We listened with humility as he stood and told us of all the *narrow shaves* that had missed sending him to destruction, near misses all the days of his life. He told us of the Cornudas rattlesnake, as he told it to me that day in the corral. He let us know how he'd ducked gunfire in Dodge City and Abilene, Kansas; and nearly joined up with the Dalton boys in Coffeyville, but didn't because he knew his wife back in Texas wouldn't like it. *Lord, what a narrow shave!* Once, back here in New Mexico, he'd almost got pecked to death by eagles in the Organ mountains. How while driving cattle down a river they thought was the Rio Grande, damned if they found out it wasn't. It was the Gila, flowing straight down to California west side of the Colorado River; and how if they hadn't found out their mistake in time they'd have landed finally in the Golden State by the blue Pacific—and, oh my, *what a narrow shave that was!* And then he told us how he nearly got scalped by Comanches while driving a herd through the Indian Territory up the Chisholm Trail.

Well, it seemed how cattle were dropping back as the big herd of Longhorns raised dust over the ruts north, and at the time there were hostile Comanches round about, themselves and their horses painted for war, and their scalping knives honed sharp, for a sweet job of revenge on the white man for killing off their buffalo.

Well sir, it was the trail boss who told this young cowboy to ride back, pick up the strays and drive them to the main herd. And while he was scouting for such like stuff, this young cowboy rode into a camp of the red-painted devils. There must have been twenty of them, all warriors.

"I was payin' mind only to their ugly faces, them aset around a big blazing fire. At first I didn't notice the carcass of beef roastin' there in the coals and flames, and I didn't look to see the big knife that was stuck in the dirt handy so's any hungry mouth could slice off a hunk of steak or brisket. And most of all I *did* let my brand-reading eye catch the beef-hide, soft and freshly killed, hangin' on a tree next to where they chewed on their dinner. And, doggone, if the brand on that hide wasn't the Cross Bar of the stock we were drivin' up to Dodge!"

He paused in his talk, just to let us think of the nasty situation he'd ridden into.

What would you do if you were aset in your saddle, with twenty Indian braves glaring up to you, their rifles and spears and bows and arrows, them hating you because you were a bona fide United States citizen?

Would you pull your six-shooter and commence firing?

Like hell you would!

Having better sense and a way with Indians you'd do as this young cowboy did.

"Gents," the Old Boss said, "I just got down from my saddle and hitched my horse to a tree. I walked over to their circle and hunkered down as near the fire as I could get—then I picked up the knife and cut me off a hunk of beef. They said nothin', but they looked at me while I ate some dinner. I said nothin', but when I got up I went to my pony, mounted him and rode off, to pick up other strays and drive them to the herd like the trail boss aimed for me to do."

He stopped his talk long enough to fire up and give us bean-eaters the dose of retribution we needed.

"Fellers, let me tell you how *that was the mostest narrow shave* I'd ever suffered all the days of my life—"

He gave some spit to his mouth, and wetted his tongue for the blast he had in mind, while we all squirmed on our hunkers for the shame that was eating on our guiltiness.

"Until last night, when your dad-burned inhospitalities gave me to know you didn't want me in your beds, all of you except old John here, that button who saved me from the worst misery Satan in hell can pile upon folks alive on this earth—

"Gents, did you ever try to trap 'em, or scare 'em away so they won't bite, or give 'em a dose of formaldehyde or lethal spirits? Did you ever squash 'em so they can't crawl no more, or shake 'em out of your shirt, or dust 'em off from inside your pants?"

Then he moved off his stance behind the potrack and came to me with his hand outstretched.

"John," he said, "by your hospitality last night you saved me from a fate worse than smallpox. *Boy, you gave me my biggest and bestest narrow shave.* Because your bed, of all the beds in this sorry camp, is the only one that ain't crawlin' lousy."

Fourteen
The Rawhiders

It's a well known fact, a lament handed down by bowlegged father to equally bowlegged son, that the single historic event that dampened and smeared the color of the West was the introduction of barbed wire, that creation of Satan.

Tailormade for "wire-cutting" valuable horse stock, for lacerating the anatomy of honest ranchfolk, and, worst of all, for breaking up the open range into compact pastures suitable for country squires on the blue grass of Kentucky, it was invented and patented in 1874 by J. F. Glidden, a Texas cattleman who had his own ranch near Amarillo fenced with the wicked strands by 1882. A drift fence (a straight line enclosing no pasture but merely a check for drifting cattle) had extended across the Texas Panhandle before that date. New Mexico, the most blessed among the territories of the Union, retained its open range long after Texas got itself entangled in barbs.

But what was used before the invention of bendable wire? Rawhide—crackly, smelly, long-lasting, wonderful rawhide of the West!

In the 1920s it seemed everybody in New Mexico still had a supply of beef hides around their ranches and places—hanging on the fences, stacked in sheds, ever-drying with hair on and tails complete. Their fresh beef had been dressed and eaten long before—and sooner or later a need would come for what remained.

To make a beef hide into pliable rawhide was to soak it in a washtub of water or in the mud of a tank down the gully for a few days until it could be pulled out, reeking and slimy, the nastiest, wettest thing on earth.

In those days anything made of or related to rawhide was artistically rough, primitively beautiful. Once the hide was out of the tub a sharp knife could be put to work. Hide that was tough as sheet iron was now soft and pliable. The edges were trimmed and the tail cut off. The flat surface was ready for cutting into desired strips or squares for making sundry articles for use around the ranch.

My rough use for rawhide was for thongs to bind corral rails or make gates and their hinges without the use of nails. When the thongs dried after a few days, they contracted to such an extent that the hold was strong and permanent. Some people scraped the hair off, using liquid solutions made from natural plants they knew of, a process used perhaps for a couple hundred years by their forebears in Texas, the Ozarks or the Blue Ridge, or right here in New Mexico. And the result was rawhide, still wet, with the texture of soft leather.

True craftsmen fashioned strips into 30-foot lariat ropes, braiding them like the hair of a damsel. Or six-foot bull-whips. Tubs, buckets, chests and trunks, nosebags and feed troughs could be made of rawhide. A hundred other uses, until baling wire, manufactured leather goods, and metal farm utensils came along and put the rough and durable rawhide out of fashion.

And it was a very special person who had an appreciation of rawhide. A person as rugged as the commodity. Yet sensitive to the artistry of its use.

I first became acquainted with the material in 1923, a month after I arrived to settle in Roswell. In September of that year I had an urge to look at El Paso. The only route out of town then was by rail northeast to Clovis with a change there, then west to Vaughn, then the Southern Pacific south to the border town. No bus line that I knew of went directly west, and what today is US 70—west to Hondo, Mescalero, Tularosa and Alamogordo—was a horrendous stretch of rutted dirt, ankle deep in dust when dry, a slosh of mud after a rain.

Someone told me that the best route to El Paso was by way of the wagon yard on South Main Street, where traveling salesmen often parked their Model Ts and welcomed company for the drive to their various destinations. All I needed to do was ask for a ride. This was the wide, bright friendly West. All traveling salesmen here wore smiling faces.

At the wagon yard I found no sign of a Model T, but there beside the corrals were three large stationary covered wagons—each the genuine article. Close to the center wagon was a campfire tended by three or four women, all in ankle-length soiled gowns, barefooted, sunbonneted. And one look at their chins indicated they were enjoying snuffdips. Two skillets were nestled in the coals, one bubbling with greens and potlikker, the other frying hog fatback. Hunks of corn pone sat in the dirt, keeping warm by their proximity to the fire.

A dozen horses munched on hay in a railed pen behind the wagons, the rails strewn with hanging travel paraphernalia, such as harness, saddles, and the family wash drying in the sun. Infants could be heard wailing in the wagons, children in two or three groups were playing in the powdery horse manure, a few with dirty faces glowering at my approach. A half-dozen men sat around a pile of firewood, chewing tobacco and spitting ambeer at the axe.

"Howdy," said one of the men, a dead-ringer for Devil Anse Hatfield.

When I asked if any salesmen in Model Ts were around, all six looked at me as though my head was ailing. But when I explained my purpose, hoping for a ride to El Paso, they looked at each other, did some spitting and apparently came to the conclusion I was sane after all.

"Nope," said a lanky one, "there ain't."

By the glint in his eye, the kind of squint used for sighting a shotgun, he could have been a McCoy.

"If you want a ride," offered Devil Anse, "we got plenty room."

"Are you going to El Paso?" I asked.

He hesitated before giving an answer. One didn't ask questions of strangers anywhere west of the Pecos, even in that late period of history. It was a lesson I had yet to learn. But they debated, looking at each other with inquiring eyes, until one spoke up and said, "Nope. We ain't. We ain't goin' that far."

"Muscular," spoke up the spit-and-image of Devil Anse, although most spit was being fired at the axe. "We'll take you that far for six-bits."

Even in my greenhorn ignorance I suspected "Muscular" meant Mescalero. In later years I concluded they had been homesteaders bound for the Sacramento Mountain country south of Mescalero and Whitetail. Nor were the six men, three women and sullied children the only party members. I saw feminine eyes watching my presence from around the canvas covers of the wagons, and a few men sleeping in sundry positions around the wheels—one snoring like a swarm of killer bees.

I declined the offer for a ride. The train would be far more satisfactory, even if I had to change at Clovis and Vaughn.

"Suit yourself," Devil Anse said, obviously hating to lose a fare of seventy-five cents and giving the axe a comet of tobacco juice.

At the hotel they told me the best and quickest way to get to El Paso would be to take a stand, or better sit, beside the road about a mile west, and flag down a salesman—one would show up sooner or later. So early the next morning I checked out with my suitcase. The September sun was hot as the hinges, and after an hour or more I decided I was out of luck—no vehicle of any traction had met or passed me as I hoped and waited.

Then, a cloud of dust rose from the roadbed at the edge of town; soon three covered wagons approached, westbound. Could it be my old friends of the wagon yard? It was.

The wagon driven by Devil Anse was the first to pull up beside me, loaded with women and children. Two redbone hound dogs came up to sniff at my suitcase, one I had bought in Glasgow, Scotland, only nine months before. The McCoy-looking driver of the second wagon followed suit, likewise the third. Two younger men were up on saddle ponies herding a half-dozen or so horses of varied colors, surprisingly fat and slick. They were riding stock of the kind familiar to Texas and New Mexico. I noticed more hound dogs bringing up the rear. Household and farm necessities, along with other women and children, cargoed the wagons of lesser importance—for Devil Anse was without doubt captain of the cavalcade.

He spit a charge of tobacco juice in my direction, not intending to hit. "Need a ride?" he said.

"Where are you going?" I asked, the same inquiry I made at the wagon yard the day before.

"Muscular," he said. "Git up here. We'll take you that far for six-bits. We'll feed you and give you a blanket for the night."

Fair enough, so the woman sitting beside Anse on the driver's seat slid back into the wagon to make room for me. Anse fired a shot of ambeer at the team and I found myself moving westward to adventure.

"My name's McAlister," Anse said, holding out a hand for me to shake. "We come from Oklahomy."

McAlister! The name had a homey sound to the ears of a new arrival from Scotland.

I thought, could this man beside me actually be a descendant of the great clan Macalister of Isla and Kintyre, whose gallant chieftain more than 450 years before was *Iain Dubh*—Black John? It was a fact in the history of the Highland clans drummed into me as a small boy in Scotland by sundry aunts and relatives. Could it possibly be?

Quite possible, for the history books tell us that at the time of the

"Clearances" following the Battle of Culloden in 1746, the Highland chiefs banished the poverty-stricken crofters, or small farmers, from their lands, even though they were kinsmen and bore their surnames. The aim was to depopulate the glens and islands and lease the heather pastures to wealthy Lowland and English lords for sheep and cattle grazing. The Clearances, like the Massacre of Glencoe, are blots on Scottish history—as was the Trail of Tears on this nation, and a hundred other crimes perpetrated against American Indians.

Thousands of the exiled Highlanders left their ancestral homes to pioneer in Nova Scotia (New Scotland), other parts of Canada, and the British colonies that later were to be the United States. The white population of North Carolina in 1760 comprised 45,000 English, 40,000 Scots, 15,000 German and 31,000 blacks, the latter all slaves. The Scots were the only large segment that came directly from their native land, settling the Cape Fear Valley. But being mountaineers, they looked to the Blue Ridge, the Great Smokies, the rugged highlands and valleys that chained down through western South Carolina and eastern Tennesee, later to the Ozarks and Ouachitas of Arkansas and Oklahoma. Many were backward and lazy, others were industrious enough to become owners and overseers of plantations all over the South. And as it was custom for slaves to take the surnames of their white masters, it stands to reason why so many of the black community today have Scottish surnames.

Through the nineteenth century and early decades of the twentieth, settlers poured out of the South to settle in Texas and New Mexico. Some of the Scots blocked up huge ranches, obtained financial backing in Scotland—and resulted in such companies as managed by John Clay of the Swan Cattle Company of Wyoming; the Prairie Cattle Company of New Mexico and Colorado, the largest cattle ranch in America; and the Matador of Texas, managed by Murdo Mackenzie with a head office in Dundee, Scotland. John Chisum, the Cattle King of New Mexico, was of Scot-plantation stock, so was Davy Crockett.

The first "range boss" in the history of Texas was Ewan Cameron, who, because of his derring-do ended his life before a firing squad in the deserts of Old Mexico.

And as Scotsmen are clansmen, and blood is thicker than water, and I was only nine months out of Scotland, I had the feeling of pride to know that I was sitting on the same wagon seat with a man named McAlister. And I told my new-found friend how I felt.

"My mama and daddy told us we was Black Dutch," was the only satisfaction I received.

But McAlister of the wagon *did* have a spark of infatuation with his name, as I soon found out. The cavalcade had come out of the mountains of eastern Oklahoma, he told me—and did I know that there is a town in that state called McAlister? Home of the state penitentiary?

He spat a comet of ambeer to the breeze as he said, "I *sure* would like to go see that electric chair, if them fellers there would let me in." Just to satisfy tourist curiosity, I presumed, not for any really practical reason.

I spent two days and a night with the McAlisters and learned a lot for my six-bits fare. We made camp for the night between Border and Picacho Hill, and made the descent of the latter early the next day. I rode with them to Hondo at the junction of the Bonito and Ruidoso rivers, where good board and lodging was available at the store, operated by a family named Rose—another Scottish clan surname that made me feel at home. There I met a salesman who gave me a lift to Alamogordo, where I caught the train to El Paso.

The covered wagon ride and night-camp near the top of Picacho Hill was an experience I have never forgotten, still vivid after fifty-eight years. The campfire in the crescent made by the three wagons was tended by women who cooked the supper—everything fried except for the cold corn pone and coffee. One skillet bubbled with okra deep in grease, another sizzled with thick slices of fatback, or salt pork.

The chief McAlister and I dined a short distance from the rest of the party. (Being a stranger, I couldn't be trusted around the women.) I suspected the wagons contained an arsenal of shotguns, rifles and ammunition, which gave me an uncomfortable feeling. Every time I glanced toward the campfire I seemed to see McAlister's trigger finger twitch. Which was not at all necessary, for under her sunbonnet each lady had a face that would stop a clock. And it was amazing to note that every member of the party, from the youngest towhead to the eldest crone, regardless of sex, when not sleeping or eating, held a chew of Brown's Mule snug in the jaw or a snuff-dip under the lip. A couple of the older women smoked on little clay pipes.

And there at the campsite my education in the use of rawhide began. On observation it seemed everything they had was made or repaired with rawhide. And the workmanship was beautiful, true artistry. When they unloaded a wagon to rearrange the contents under the bows and canvas, I noticed what appeared to be a bathtub-sized vat, although I'm sure it had no relation to the familiar bathroom fixture. Bathing was not for these people. But the craftsmen who made it must have had a spark of delicacy somewhere—the smoothing of the rawhide and lacing of the seams was superbly done.

There were rawhide stools and pails, large squares tough and smooth that served as dining tables when placed on the ground, or for infants to kick and prattle on in the shade under the wagons. Repairs on all parts of the wagons were done by the use of "whangs," strips of rawhide tightly wrapped around a break in the coupling-pole or tongue, even the wheelspokes—put on wet and allowed to dry and contract to a permanent bind, a hold that would last for the life of the wagon.

There was one piece of furniture that took my eye, a chicken coop under the wagon beside the "reach," held secure by rawhide braces. I admired the workmanship and let McAlister know about it.

"That there chicken coop nigh bust our hearts," he said. "They was all fightin' roosters, the meanest and best in Oklahomy."

"Did they break out and get lost?" I asked, wondering why so fine a coop was without chickens.

McAlister shook his head and gulped for the thought I had brought to mind. It was indeed a sad tale he told. It seems that, coming down off the Kiamichi foothills the roosters were healthy, happy and crowing, secure in their coop. Until the cavalcade reached the Red River. Most civilized people crossed that boundary stream between Oklahoma and Texas by the bridge south of Durant and north of Denison, but the McAlisters chose to cut mileage by fording the water a goodly distance to the west and to get stuck midstream in the process. It took them a full hour to reach the Texas shore. McAlister's grief was genuine, for there is no sight more dismal than a coopful of drowned chickens.

Another fixture nailed to the wagon side was a rawhide chest with the hair left on, measuring about 30 inches long, 16 high and a foot wide, neatly and firmly laced with whangs. It was a toolbox, strong and everlasting. McAlister showed me how it was made. In later years, when taking up residence in a cabin north side of the Capitan mountains, where a packhorse was necessary for freighting supplies, I made two *alforjas*, or packboxes, according to his instructions. I found two orange crates of the desired size, which I bound around with flat wet rawhide, hair side out. Holes were punched along the seams and laced with wet rawhide strips. Two loops were attached to an upper side, measured right to hang on the packsaddle prongs. When the rawhide had dried and contracted and the orange crates were smashed to splinters and pulled out, I had two matching boxes, one for each side of the horse. Through the ensuing years I packed home many a slab of bacon and pound of Arbuckle's coffee from Titsworth's store in Capitan in my rawhide *alforjas*.

Now the sun has set and the mountains to the west are cobalt against the fiery red sky, the lower grassy flats are spread with an amethyst sheet. Beside a murky water hole, the first wagon stops, the second pulls up and is followed by the other to form a circle.

After supper, there may be music. Mountain music. Fiddle tunes and ballads handed down over the centuries.

The Rawhiders—they were a separate culture among us. They came from the hills of the South, mountain people ever on the move westward. They traveled in covered wagons, twelve to fifteen vehicles in a party, and always with a remuda. They dispensed with cattle for two reasons—the herd would become trailworn and, besides, other people's stock were ever available for butchering. Or for branding of mavericks or dogies to be sold for cash.

The Rawhiders earned the name by their thousand-and-one uses of rawhide—and the dried hides of stolen and slaughtered cattle that filled the wagon beds.

They crossed the Llano Estacado into New Mexico, where they found ripe hunting grounds on the huge ranches. Their wagons stretched out for miles on the way west—west, ever westward, to the farthest limits of the territory.

The men were gaunt, stone-faced, silent for long stretches of time, but rough and rude and loud when they had occasion to talk, their language their own, Elizabethan in its color and accent.

The women were the barefoot kind. Marriages were quick and easy, and widows didn't hold that status for long. The youngters were many, born in the rolling wagons. Burials were made as the train looked to the horizon ahead, with perhaps a small cairn of rocks left to mark the spot.

Without schooling, the Rawhider was a wizard at reading and writing—reading and altering other folk's brands, that is.

The Rawhiders were a tradition, American—not as apple pie but rather as corn pone, greens and pot likker. The rawhide era gone, most settled down to be honest homesteaders.

Fifteen
Packhorse to Plumb Paradise

Back in 1928, Old Man Charlie Dixon ran a bunch of cows on the south side of the Capitan Mountains, up against The Gap in Lincoln County, and I lived opposite on the north side. I lived in a log cabin on 160 acres of fenced pasture, along with three saddle horses—a black, a sorrel and a dun—several cats and about twenty-three chickens, nice blue Andalusians that I bought from Old Man Charlie Dixon.

The cats kept the cabin clean of pack rats, the chickens laid me eggs, and I used the saddle horses for periodic trips to short jobs whenever they opened up, on ranches close by or off a ways. It didn't matter which. It was the way a bachelor-cowboy liked to live.

And when the wages were earned, I packhorsed into Capitan for stocking the cabin with supplies. Twenty dollars' worth of groceries would last me a couple months.

My horses, cats and poultry shared the same contentment along with Old Man Charlie Dixon's cattle, which grazed off to the Block Ranch pastures—much to the displeasure of Lloyd Taylor, the Block foreman. I rented the cabin and horse pasture from Old Man Charlie Dixon for five dollars a month, or sixty dollars for a full year.

One day in the spring of 1928, which was a dry one, Old Man Charlie Dixon came over across Capitan Gap to pay me a visit and say howdy. He rode a bay pony, and his white hair was nested under a big hat without a crease in it, and his long white mustache was bright in the sun. His saddle was plain-stamped, his chaps without conchas, his spurs sort of rusty and his boots lacked fancy stitching. He was of the Texas cattleman breed and hated fooferaw. The stove was hot so we drank some Arbuckle's.

"John," said Old Man Charlie Dixon, after we'd set ourselves by the cast-iron stove on nail kegs cushioned with gunnysacks, "I'm here to give you an invite."

I couldn't figure what kind of invite Old Man Charlie Dixon had in mind, but if it was a fried chicken dinner cooked by his wife, that kind of invite was all right with me. I could have done with some chicken, because I'd had sourdough biscuits and water-and-lard gravy for breakfast, with pepper and salt to make it tasty, and I was sorely in need of a change of feed. But it wasn't that kind of invite.

"John," he went on, "do you know you don't need to die and go to heaven for to be happy in paradise, cause paradise is right here on earth."

"Where?" I demanded.

"Bingham, New Mexico," he said. "It's t'other side of the Carrizozo malpais."

I knew exactly where Bingham was. I'd crossed the Carrizozo lava beds on two previous occasions, once in 1924 on a trip to San Marcial on the Rio Grande from Roswell, riding with a friend in his Model T touring car. Then again, in the spring of 1926, when my pony and myself went off riding chuck line.

I loved San Marcial. In all my years since that time, anywhere in the state, I have never come upon a more sun-blessed little town than that by the river just north of Elephant Butte Lake.

Someday, I used to think, San Marcial will be my home.

But so help me, never could I find anything heavenly about Bingham, except that Bingham was not too far from San Marcial.

To me, San Marcial, with its sunshine and the creosote perfume from the railroad, was the epitome of all that set New Mexico apart from the rest of the nation.

There were shops, a bank, an opera house and a Harvey House where men from the Santa Fe roundhouse and yards and station enjoyed meals that only a Harvey House could provide. There was freshness in the air from the cottonwoods along the river bank. Railroad men mixed with cowboys on the street, along with gingham-gowned wives. Children were in country-style quantity, for San Marcial was a *family* town. Harmony, fellowship, hospitality, social pride and decency were there under a brilliant therapeutic sun.

The wide sweep of surrounding desert was New Mexican to the letter—places with lilting Spanish names like the Fra Cristobal Mountains to the south, the San Mateo range faraway westward. Off to the east ranged the Sierra Oscura, the dark obscure mountains. And between the Oscuras and the Fra Cristobals lay that ninety-mile desert stretch—New Mexico's famous Jornada del Muerto, Route of the Dead Man.

Old Man Charlie Dixon and I warmed ourselves on the Arbuckle's. The cast-iron stove gave out its heat in tune with the aroma of piñon.

"Yes," I said, "I know where Bingham is. I passed it by twice and both times in a hurry."

"You're wrong what you're thinkin', John," Old Man Charlie Dixon said, accusingly. "Bingham is beautiful. It's *plumb paradise*."

Then I heard what the old man had in mind, what the invite was all about.

"John," he said, "Have you ever thought of havin' a sweet little ranch of your own, cattle of your own, no more huntin' for jobs or sleepin' in stinkin' bunkhouses?"

Had I! Days and nights I had dreamed of a clean little twenty-section outfit—somewhere and someday. One that would graze maybe 300 mother cows, not too deep down to water, where I could sit in the saddle and admire a windmill with a sixteen-foot wheel hoisting a blessing up to the storage tank and cattle troughs. A good spread of grama grass everywhere, and arroyos for winter shelter, and possibly a few cedar breaks. A good set of corrals in the right places, each with a windmill to make it pretty. A fine string of saddle-ponies, good of action with sense in the brain. Nothing fancy, but of the little Spanish cowpony breed. Registered hereford bulls that by simple biology would increase the quality of the stock. A glistening new Model T touring car, or better a truck—maybe a Reo Speed Wagon. A forty-acre horse trap next to the corrals at headquarters. And a neat white frame ranch house with a pitched roof and plenty of "gallery" to it.

I never dreamed of having wifely companionship in that ranch house, but of one thing I was sure—whenever I moved I'd take along the three saddle ponies, my cats, and my blue Andalusian chickens.

"I know the place," Old Man Charlie Dixon said, draining a mug of Arbuckle's, "and it's down there south of Bingham—maybe fifteen or twenty miles. It's got Oscura Peak at its east boundary. And Lord! What a spread of grass! Not too deep down to water, and the winters ain't so iced-up like they are round here.

"There's plenty open country, just right for filing 640-acre claims. I've got my homesteadin' rights, so have you. We can file on a section apiece, you

Chapter Fifteen

and me. That will give us 1,280 acres patented after we prove up. From there on we'll start blocking up sections—and before we know it we'll have land and cattle."

I began licking my teeth for such a tasty thought.

"Where would we go for stocking up on supplies?" I asked.

"Carrizozo," he said. "Maybe Socorro, but Geronimo Baca's big mercantile store in San Marcial would be the nearest."

San Marcial!

Could I be hearing it straight from Old Man Charlie Dixon, or was I in heaven getting the truth from the Angel Gabriel?

"When can we go?" I said, pouring Arbuckle's. "Because I *sure* want to see that country."

"Any time," said Old Man Charlie Dixon. "You've got horses, so have I. And I'll tell you again, John, that there territory is *plumb paradise*."

It was a sundown in late May when Old Man Charlie Dixon came over the Gap riding his bay horse. The saddle strings held a gunnysack of chuck-makings behind the cantle. Like flour and a bucket of lard, five packages of Arbuckle's coffee, salt and a fifteen-pound smoked ham, brown and pretty, that he'd bought for fifteen cents a pound. He'd stay all night in my cabin and we'd leave together with four horses before sunrise the next morning. I would ride the dun, put the loaded packsaddle on the black, while the little flax-maned sorrel could trot along with my bed in the canvas tarp squaw-hitched over his back and girth.

My big contribution to the camp menu was a twenty-pound slab of prime bacon I'd bought at Titsworth's store in Capitan for four dollars. It was high-price, and it seemed like I was providing three horses to his one, nearly all the load on the packsaddle, and giving him half my bed. But I realized, too, that he'd paid out $2.25 for the ham. And most important—his part in the trip was showing me the way to Paradise.

We took off by the light of the morning star and headed northwest for White Oaks. The bed horse and packhorse were trotting sweetly ahead of us, the pack secured with a diamond hitch. It takes two men to throw a diamond hitch, the best for holding power, but if a man travels alone he has to rely on a simpler squaw hitch. I'd cooked up a three-week supply of lard gravy to leave for the cats, and I put out a half-bushel of corn chops for the chickens.

Nobody west of the hundredth meridian locked their doors in those days, so I left mine to be opened should someone come by to cook a meal and stay all night. I was sorry I had to take my bed and skillet with us on the trip. I figured we'd be gone about three weeks. The guest could bed down on the floor.

We made camp and hobbled the horses past sundown of every evening, selecting a place near water and on a good turf of grass. From White Oaks our course was round the north end of the Carrizozo lava beds and south of the Chupadera Mesa. We'd hit Bingham from the east. It was only a forty-mile buzzard flight from Bingham to San Marcial, closer yet from Plumb Paradise, and no distance at all to the grocery store if we went by the Model T or the Reo Speed Wagon of my dreams.

The days were getting pretty hot, although the nights were still cool. We hadn't put our ponies to more than a trot since we left the Capitans. Many hours of the way we rode at a slow walk—did lots of getting down off the saddles, stretching out to doze in the spring sunlight while the horses nibbled on the dry grass. By the time we passed Bingham with only a howdy, it was late in the evening, and we reached the final mile of our journey to Plumb Paradise when dark had already taken the Jornada.

We made camp and built a fire, hobbled our horses. And out in the darkness to the east of us Oscura Peak rose in its somberness toward the starlit sky.

Have you ever sat next to a campfire of stinking desert scrubwood listening to an old Texas cattleman tell of his younger years, and all the cattle and horses and grass and waterings that comprised the glory of San Saba County? He sat there on his hunkers, nursing a mug of Arbuckle's, his big uncreased hat straight up on his downy head, his eyes glistening with memories of times when Texas was younger and cleaner, more open—and when Young Man Charlie Dixon rode high in the saddle and was part of the scene.

"I tell you, John, them were heavenly days, and sometimes I wish to hell I'd never come West."

But now, in the month of June in 1928, if San Saba County was paradise lost, here on the Jornada for the old cowboy was paradise about to be gained.

We were out of the tarp-bed at the rise of the morning star. It shone bigger and brighter than usual while it blazed the trail of daylight over the Oscura range. We kindled a fire. Big thick slices of ham and bacon browned in the skillet and we were fixed to make pan-bread in the grease. And while God made the morning Old Man Charlie Dixon and me made Arbuckle's coffee and poured molasses on our plates, and drowned it with bacon grease, and looked around us. Now Plumb Paradise shone like jewelry spread out to make glory of the clear New Mexico sky.

There stood Oscura Peak, all right, its summit high on the east horizon. Far to the west stretched the Fra Cristobals and the Rio Grande. The yucca grew tall on bristly legs. There were stink-gourds round about, the staghorn cactus grew on thick trunks with spines on its branches to maintain dignity.

But help me if I'm wrong, except for its magnificent desolation, its wildness and solitude, its horizons that stretched from pole to pole, seemingly from ocean to ocean, and the romance of its very name—I couldn't see anything economically interesting in the paradise Old Man Charlie Dixon found. And for a fact, I hated the thought of any human being, including Old Man Charlie Dixon and me, showing his presence to uglify the God-sculptured scene around us.

"Don't you reckon somebody's got this country already?" I asked.

"Likely," said Old Man Charlie Dixon. "But there's plenty sections open for homesteadin', and enough state and federal territory for leasin'. We can find out about all that maybe next year sometime, when we can git a feller with an automobile to take us to the Land Office in Las Cruces. Leave it to me, John, then all this rich grazin' will be our ranch, yours and mine."

Rich grazing!

Well, hell!

We saddled up for a trot of inspection around Plumb Paradise. We killed three rattlesnakes in the four-hour excursion. And when we got back to camp I was all set to make pony tracks back to the north side of the Capitans where my cats and chickens, and my sweet little log house were enjoying their place on earth.

What we saw was the Jornada del Muerto in the heat of June. We saw lots of cactus and yucca, some sotol and agave, all kinds of desert weeds, and darn little grass. But June is dry in New Mexico, everywhere, and maybe with the rains of August this faraway scope of territory would freshen up, come alive.

There would be varmints all around, like coyotes and bobcats—pure hell on my cats and chickens. There'd be funny kinds of lizards and bullsnakes. Any house built here would be home sweet home for tarantulas and spiders. There'd be hydrophoby cats (rabid skunks). To find water we'd have to drill down to Alice Springs, Australia. The range would carry about five mother cows to the section, and then try to starve them to death. And here, as we'd already found out, rattlesnakes slithered in wholesale quantities and grew to Texas-size lengths and diameters.

And here's a fact sad to remember. As Old Man Charlie Dixon unsaddled his pony, I noticed a look of disappointment in the eyes under that big Stetson hat.

But San Marcial was still shining in its glory, wasn't it, some forty miles southwest? The Harvey girls in the restaurant would be feeding the railroadmen dinner, and cowboys were on the street standing in groups talking their own kind of language.

"There," said I to myself, "is Plumb Paradise. And someday San Marcial will be my home."

The heat of June blasted our camp that midday of our disappointment, the intense farenheit of it, the blistering dryness.

And while Old Man Charlie Dixon cooked our noon meal on a fire of desert scrub—boiled prunes and greased pan-bread—San Andres Peak and the Caballo Mountains were ashen in the sun-glare, the mesas next to Skillet Knob heaved and quivered, the rattlers sought shade and the coyotes buried their presence up and down the sandy arroyos.

We saddled up and rode north from Plumb Paradise, Old Man Charlie Dixon and me. Our bed-horse and pack pony trotted in front of us, their horse sense telling them they were heading home, home where my blue Andalusian chickens were ranging around, hunting bugs, where the cats were getting fat on pack rats, where maybe somebody had, while I horsed off to Paradise, stopped by and put his pony in the pasture, cooked himself a supper and stayed all night.

On reaching home I found everything exactly as I expected. Old Man Charlie Dixon rode off for his ranch south-side of the Gap. He packed along what was left of the ham, I hung the remains of the bacon slab high on the rafters. And doggone if there wasn't a note propped on the table against the coal-oil lamp—a note scribbled with the same pencil on the same pad as I used for writing my stories: *Friend John I stayd all nit.*

And so he had, but he left no name. It didn't matter. He was just the unknown cowboy. He had fried some eggs and baked a few biscuits, although he didn't bother to boil any dried peaches. He had washed the dishes like a gentleman. He must have slept on his saddle blanket and used his saddle for a pillow. And after he rode away my fine spare bridle with the Kelly bits was hanging on its nail safe and sound, and my best Saturday-go-to-Roswell Stetson that was up there next to it. If I had had a bucket of silver dollars open on the table, there for the taking, I could be assured that nary a one would be found missing—although the Good Lord knows my supply of any kind of dollar was mighty slim. But that was the way of the New Mexico ranch country back in those years. Hospitality was everywhere, and it was to be respected. Padlocked doors were nowhere to be found.

Old Man Charlie Dixon seldom talked about our trip to Plumb Paradise. He'd come by to eat dinner with me once in a while, and inspect his cattle ranging around. We'd eat fried potatoes and beans, maybe a fried egg, and if I'd boiled some prunes we'd have prunes. He talked a lot of his early years in San Saba County, one anecdote after another, about big-hatted, white-mustached cowmen like himself, precious words to the ears of a hopeful writer.

"You know, John," he'd say, nursing his cup of Arbuckle's, "anywhere you go in Texas, it's plumb paradise."

Too bad the packhorse trail to the desert west of Oscura Peak didn't pay out. But I still was primed with ambition, to make San Marcial my home some sweet day.

For a year after that, when riding sometimes down to Carrizozo, ahorseback, I'd look off to the west, and I'd see Oscura Peak raised dark in the distance, and know that beyond that lonely mountain lay Old Man Charlie Dixon's Plumb Paradise. And southwest of there, God bless it, was San Marcial.

I thought of the town most especially in June in 1929, when the rains had come extra early, greening up the Carrizozo and Patos mountains, and the whole Capitan range glistened with freshness and grass and plant-growth—so different from the past year's June when Old Man Charlie Dixon and I took our trip, full of hope and dreams and faith.

This year, I told myself, I'd packhorse down there again, me and my horses. And I'd get someone with a truck to haul the plunder—the cats in a cage and the chickens in a coop. And nobody in God's world, wild horses or stampeding cattle, would drive me away from San Marcial.

I planned on October for the move. The best month, when the country would be cooling down.

And while I dreamed and planned lightning cracked in the high Capitans, and the summer rains were falling all over New Mexico.

In August, I rode chuck line with the flax-maned sorrel to ranches on the north side of the mountain—just to say howdy and help as needed.

I was in White Oaks August 14, the day the news came.

The news said how the clouds hung low over the mountains and flats east and west of the Rio Grande, and the river valley was an ocean-size mixture of water, silt and muck. Water flowing from the Jemez, the San Mateos, the Sangre de Cristos. Water down the Rio Puerco and Rio Salado—until Elephant Butte Lake filled to overloading and backed up the river.

The deluge had been most destructive over the weekend and into Monday. A special Santa Fe train arrived in San Marcial at nine in the morning of Tuesday to evacuate 200 women and children, while the men worked feverishly sandbagging the weakening dikes. Merchants and residents had transported their belongings to higher ground and camped out in the midst of them to watch their homes and business establishments being devoured by the water. By noon of the thirteenth every adobe house in town was lost, including the Methodist Church. Only the roundhouse and Harvey House remained standing, along with the bank and a few stores and railroad buildings. Some hulks that were homes stood in the water, their only purpose now to bring tears.

The people of San Marcial being a special breed, they went back to town to clean up the wreckage and rebuild.

But the Rio Grande is a treacherous companion. In late September torrential rains sent the river again over its banks.

San Marcial was gone forever.

"It don't matter none," said Old Man Charlie Dixon, drinking a cup of my Arbuckle's in the lean-to after he'd rode over the Gap to look after his cattle.

"There's still Carrizozo and Socorro for to go to the store. If San Marcial ain't there, then, well sir, it ain't there."

"That's right, Charlie," I said. "It just ain't there."

But Plumb Paradise was there—and it's there today in the sunrise shadow of Oscura Peak—the obscure, dark foreboding mountain.

If we'd claimed our homesteads, how long would they have been ours? Exactly seventeen years and one month after our packhorse trot of inspection, on the sixteenth of July in 1945, at a pre-dawn hour when most of America was deep in unsuspecting sleep, the Jornada del Muerto came awake with a shock, and a huge cloud shaped like a giant mushroom billowed over the yucca flats and the alkali sinks—over the ocotillo and sotol—a blast that rocked the world.

And Plumb Paradise became the Trinity Site.

Sixteen
Light on Dark Mountain

Of all the mountain ranges that lift their peaks to New Mexican skies, three win my nomination for the most beautiful of all—the wildest, most dramatic altars to the God of the desert, north to south arteries of sculptured crags and deep canyons, each rising abruptly from an arid floor of greasewood, cactus and mesquite. They are high places where, when the terminal hour of my life arrives, I would choose to rest and mingle ashes with sand, shale, and sunshine. Now in life they are where my heart abides, although I no longer dwell in their vicinity.

The mountain chains I refer to are the Peloncillos of far southwestern New Mexico, peaks that almost cast their shadows across the Sonora border; and the San Andres that form a rampart dividing the White Sands from the Jornada del Muerto; and the Sierra Oscura, where the culminating peak looks eastward over the black-rock Carrizozo lava beds, miles and miles in length and width, the epitome of the wild.

Of all the mountains named I am more familiar with the Oscuras, the dark companions of the sky, obscure as their Spanish name implies. In fond remembrance I see them now, as I live far to north of where I used to watch them so often astride a pony Carrizozo-bound from my home on the north side of the Capitans, through fourteen years of crossing the Bernardo Gap that cut Carrizo mountain from the Vera Cruz and the Tucsons, taking the trail down from Leo Smith's ranch and approaching Kudner's O Bar O. And how the Oscuras, then, seemed so appropriately named—dark and mysterious, obscure.

Little did I know then that a blinding light cast upon them, so near in the future, would change the course of history, and for good or ill deeply affect the lives of every human being, every living thing resident in the world. To the east of the Oscuras was Carrizozo, where Will Ed Harris was a familiar figure around town, where Paden's drug store dispensed relief in bottles for aches and pains, where Prehm's department store enticed viewers to the window by displaying exotic, sometimes shocking items of merchandise. And where the Southern Pacific Beanery served copious quality meals to men of both rail and the range.

Carrizozo—What a grand and glorious cow town it used to be!

To the west of the Oscuras the north end of the Jornada del Muerto prepares to meet the south uplift of the Chupadero Mesa, where the San Antonio-to-Carrizozo highway cuts between, where tiny Bingham basks in serenity, where the desert Old Man Charlie Dixon named "Plumb Paradise" for his own pleasure lies east of the town where Conrad Hilton was born, and where San Marcial died in the flood. The lonely obscured Sierra Oscura.

Why, oh why, would the genius of America choose to brighten them with the light that heralded an end to the world we used to know?

Santa Fe, of course, is the political heart of New Mexico, and there the engineers who control the state's destiny have their hands on the throttle. Twenty-five miles north of Santa Fe, today, is one of the new, hastily built towns of our sovereign—Los Alamos, and all the world knows how Los Alamos came to be. The beeline distance from Santa Fe Plaza to Oscura Peak covers 145 miles southward over enchanted land. The peak has a moderate altitude, 8,732 feet. Little Burro Peak, ten miles south of Oscura, a mountain that also received the Light of Lights, is a mere 7,410 feet elevation, really not much higher than Santa Fe Plaza renowned as the highest seat of state government in the nation. There is no town like Santa Fe, as any of its residents will attest, but mix Los Alamos and Oscura Peak together, and there you have a cocktail explosive enough to wreck the cities of Hiroshima and Nagasaki, and out of the poison, ashes and rubble introduce to the Lord of Creation a new civilization not akin to His own quiet, loving plan.

I was living on another desert south of Santa Fe that day when Oscura Peak took the Light, with days and nights for me, remote from Lincoln County's Cowboy Riding Country which I left eight years before. The day was July 16, 1945. World War II was raging on and all and sundry of my acquaintance were severely sick of it. It was a Monday, and I chose to spend it in Santa Fe. I arrived there just as the afternoon paper, *The New Mexican*, came off the presses—the usual wartime offering on its front page, something to skip in favor of the local news.

The La Fonda lobby was dim-lit and hushed, but the Cantina had already filled with cocktail hour socialites. A glance through the open door showed Pansy Stockton of "Sun Painting" fame at a table with Kyle Crichton just in from New York. Datus Myers was sitting in company with "BeeBee" Dunne—likewise Will Shuster of the Camino del Monte Sol, Lynn Riggs of the Acequia Madre, but I couldn't see John Sloan of East Garcia Street anywhere present—or Randall and Belle Davey of Canyon Road. Oh, the noise of them! Oh, the laughter and nasty gossip! Lulu, the Harvey Girl cocktail waitress, was distributing at the tables the nectar that cheers.

So I sought the lobby where George, the most noted bellhop on the Fred Harvey chain, was loading tourist baggage in a cart front of the registration desk hopeful of a generous tip. George, who in this same lobby had carried luggage of the crowned heads of Europe, the Orient, and of the British Dominions beyond the seas, not to forget the Gaekwar of Baroda and Lord Halifax.

The Hawkeye Agents down from Los Alamos were everywhere about, at the news stand, at the desk, even a special whose apparent beat was the "Gents." A Hawkeye Hen kept her eyes and ears open in the "Ladies." Either sex of them, they were mistrusted by everyone.

What were the eggheads doing up at Los Alamos, anyway?

What was happening at the laboratory called the Manhattan Project, an ex-alpine boys' school where once in the 1930s I attended a lively party.

Were they building a giant submarine up there?

Or was it, as a few Santa Feans thought, a sanctuary for pregnant Wacs?

The comfort of the lobby armchair was remote from the war-torn far Pacific, and the inner pages of the day's *New Mexican* provided the news I really cared for, such as the goings-on in tranquil Santa Fe. The weather bureau forecasted partly cloudy skies for the day, with possible scattered showers, a high temperature of eighty-eight and a low of fifty-four. The Lensic Theater advertised as "now showing" Sonja Henie in *It's A Pleasure*, a colossal supported by Michael O'Shea and Marie McDonald. The Safeway Stores, Inc., were offering in return for cash and ration coupons reductions in certain food items, and Moore's menswear featured in picture a gentleman nattily dressed in the fashion of 1945. Then on the society page I gave my eye to Dorothy Larson's *Paso Por Aqui* column.

There I learned that John Skolle, an artist, had just returned to Santa Fe after a short stay in New York; and that Betty Binkley, another artist and well-known Santa Fean, was home at San Sebastian Ranch after eleven months of painting at Chapala, Mexico, and that the result of the adventure was hanging in the Art Museum gallery and drawing favorable acclaim from all viewers, which it very well deserved.

Then, scanning the same page further, I noted at the very top of Dorothy's *Personal Briefs* the top feature story of the day:

> Astronomy Division: A few nights ago, Norman Appleton tells us, he was reposing happily on a couch in his patio gazing at the sky, when a comet with a tail a quarter of the way across the sky flashed right over his face. Startling, Norman says, but beautiful.

I thought: Norman must have been napping, dreaming, for comets never happen over Santa Fe. But now, I'm inclined to reconsider, it was a prelude, an overture to the most terrible drama ever staged in the history of the world.

On the very last page of that day's *New Mexican*, hidden among advertisements and Lodge notices, cramped where no one with better to do would give it a moment's notice, was this insignificant report:

> MAGAZINE LETS GO AT ALAMOGORDO
> Alamogordo, N.M., July 16—AP. An explosion of a magazine on the Alamogordo Air Base Reservation this morning, heard and seen for many miles, was reported today by William O. Eareckson, Commanding officer at the air base. There was no loss of life or injuries to persons, Eareckson said.

Now, say I, after thirty-six years, that was one terrific, public-deceiving falsehood. But that's the way of warriors and scientists, of war and physics, of dealers in death and destruction. We learned the truth on the following August 6 and 9 with the toppling and slaughter of Hiroshima and Nagasaki. And the seed of it all was sprouted in New Mexico. In Cowboy Riding Country. When the Light of the New Age was flashed on Oscura Peak.

Today a pyramid of black lava-rock stands alone and seldom seen on the floor of the Jornada del Muerto—"The Journey of the Deadman." It is a monument that marks Ground Zero, where the hundred-foot-high steel tower stood on the Day of Trinity, which cradled "The Bomb" that unleashed the Los Alamos mystery.

A metal plaque riveted to the stonework reads:

> TRINITY SITE
> Where
> The World's First
> Nuclear Device
> Was Exploded On
> July 16, 1945

They triggered the "Thing" from a reinforced bunker five miles away in the predawn while Socorro, Carrizozo, Tularosa, Hot Springs slept or was just awakening. And, it is said, the sound of the fury rattled windows in Gallup, about two hundred miles to the west. Then a ghostly brilliance took the Jornada. It flashed itself on the waters of Elephant Butte Lake, and the San Cristobal mountains were vivid in a color that can't be described. The heat melted the tower and obliterated all life—reptile, insect, vegetable—and the sand and rocks and minerals for a half-mile around the core became in an instant something not of this earth, but rather what Dante found and described in the depths of the Inferno. No one in the bunker cheered as the mushroom cloud fogged the purest starlight in the world. But, it is told, Kenneth Bainbridge, the nuclear physicist then field commander of the project, made the fateful and prophetic statement: "Now we're all sons of bitches."

And how did the giant fireball affect Cowboy Riding Country? Affect! Hell, it put the old wonderful, clean, easy-paced, friendly horseback world we knew out of business, changed the ways and thinking of ranch people, even though their ranges were hundreds of miles beyond all horizons from Ground Zero. The ground where Old Man Charlie Dixon and I hobbled our horses out for the night, as we looked around for land to homestead and block up a ranch, that night by the campfire in 1928, just west of the down-slope of Oscura Peak, when the old man said, "John, this country is Plumb Paradise." What became of it? Well, the heat of the misfortune melted the sand and every living thing upon or within, and made of it a lake of liquid glass—which cooled, refused, and hardened into trinitite, hence the name Trinity, a word quiet-thinking folk revered before the blast and in spite of it hold in reverence today.

And say, do you know the red-coated white-faced cattle grazing around Bingham had the hairs on their hides changed to white?

They say it had something to do with the air.

The sun shone sickly over the Jornada for awhile, while the air held the contamination, and starlight wasn't the kind of starlight we used to see, once thrilled by its purity and thankful that by grace of our guardian angels New Mexico was our home.

More than three-and-a-half decades have passed into history since Oscura Peak was brightened in the morning dark. Year by year new methods have invaded ranch work and living, and the old-and-tried for a hundred years have given way to a rapid, more efficient way of doing things.

The pickup truck with its familiar horse-trailer hitched behind has replaced the remuda, now when a half-dozen riders on the roundup can do the work of thirty in earlier times. The chuck-wagon is no longer needed, neither is that man of wit and color and cantankerousness—the roundup cook. Food for the boys is brought in from headquarters by pickup, prepared by the womenfolks in spotless kitchens equipped with all manner of electric doodads—the microwave quickie favored over the old time dutch oven. Propane gives fire to the branding irons now rather than the flame of cedar and oak, and even some corrals are constructed of prefabricated iron bars and placed together in sections—and as electric powerlines have reached even to the faraway ranches, the windmills with their sucker rods and high-turning wheels—each a romance portrait of the West—have been torn down, replaced with trouble-free submersible pumps. And why not, for unless the rancher does the work himself it costs $75 for an outside pump crew to even replace the leathers. For inflation is the price of progress. And the most acute change of all, the masculine world of the cattleman and his cowboys, which in former times was confined to lone camps and inconveniences that only the sturdiest male could endure, is now invaded by the horsewoman—athletic, expert, and equipped with brainpower the old cowboy mentality never enjoyed. But, alas, with her presence the romance of the range went with the rolling tumbleweed into history, to the writing of memoirs, to ride not on grass or along hoof-worn trails, but on the printed page and the brushstrokes of artists who try to revive it for the sake of present and future generations. All that, and the magnificent preservation of it at the National Cowboy Hall of Fame and Western Heritage Center, high on Persimmon Hill in Oklahoma City.

Yet, Cowboy Riding Country today is an island in a vast sea of American progress, much of it remote from business conveniences and touch-button devices. The horseback outlaw of old, who ever flirted with the posse and hangrope, has been replaced by personalities with equal greed but less daring; even the God-given grass, the fuel that engineered every phase of work on the ranch, space and time that was profit for the owner and livelihood of the bowlegged, sun-blistered wage earner, now has been usurped by developers who couldn't care less for any life or hard-won endeavor, of beauty or things natural and clean, his purpose only to satisfy his fabricated idea of bringing in the urban alien drift that would people and make complete the destructive work of his bulldozer—tempt the privacy of people who love their West, their plains and their valleys and canyons, who were there when the West needed men and women to "match my mountains," and stayed with their accomplishments throughout the generations.

In spite of the condominium on the horizon there are cowtowns remaining in West Texas, New Mexico and Arizona, where men who qualify them for distinction against any other in all America as "home on the range"—unchanged, out in the boondocks, wide places on the highway, where white-haired old men and their youth with the sun-squinted eyes hunker down on the "galleries" that front truly rustic places of business, or in rocking chairs as they relive the grand, the glorious years gone by in talk or silent memory. There are thousands alive and at work in Cowboy Riding Country. Look to Magdalena, to Corona, to Hachita, to Hillsboro, to Fairbank, to the tangle of cactus and mesquite that used to be the Bloody Basin—and there you will find them.

Two of these great pioneers are most prominent in my own private estimation—one a woman, as gallant as Western womanhood ever was made. She lives in the ghost town of Shakespeare, two short miles out of Lordsburg, and her name is Rita Hill. She and her daughter are the only residents and all that was once the roaring camp of a hundred years ago is their property, their home to love and preserve. Together they live in the splendor of the early-day West, without electricity, sacrificing the gadgets of less stalwart women, living a life that is gone for others but theirs by grace of their own intelligence. And they are as defiant as any of their forebears, whose defiance built the West—and woe betide any developer who would blemish the sanctity of their home and surroundings.

A few years ago the New Mexico State Highway Department sought to build a cloverleaf for a junction along Interstate 10 a short distance west of Lordsburg, and by power of eminent domain would condemn for the purpose a section of her cattle range. She was given notice—an insult to her pride, to her commitment of preserving the lovely against the encroachment of the unlovely. There happened to be a shack on the property condemned, and in this Rita Hill immediately took residence, while her daughter cared for old Shakespeare and brought meals and necessities to the battle front.

Rita Hill stayed in the shack for weeks until the bulldozers and dump trucks moved in. And when the construction crews tried to evict her she showed the defiance of all the courageous women of history—Annie Oakley, Joan of Arc, Calamity Jane, Betsy Ross and sundry others—but the quality of Rita Hill in particular. It was only when the overpowering law officers of Lordsburg arrived to handcuff her, almost drag her away, did she lose her fight. She was a citizen of Shakespeare, where a hundred years ago men were hanged for the crime of "being a damned nuisance." Luckily for the State Highway Department it wasn't in existence then.

Another who defied the encroachment of the usurpers upon his home and fireside was one old man, aged but with all the ingredients of an iron will, a ranchman of the Alamogordo area—John Prather by name. His house and range lay west of the town, spreading over a once quiet expanse of New Mexico desert, his cattle and horses subsisting on scant forage in view of the Organ mountains to the west, the Sacramentos at the east. And, with white hair showing under his Stetson hat, John Prather was a valiant, highly intelligent man on horseback. But he, because of the cravings of warriors of the recently terminated Great War of the World, had an adversary—this the Command of the Armed Forces of the United States of America. And darned if the high brass didn't yearn with vigor to evict him, to possess his ranch for a range of their own, not a range for grazing cattle, but upon which to fire off rockets of destruction, to be part of the White Sands Missile Range, the same that contained the deadly Trinity Site at its very north end.

But John Prather being the man he was, he unflinchingly met the uniformed colonels whose intent was to serve him with papers, they requesting a signature that would transfer for a price his home, his living and his life, to the Government that cared little for anything he held sacred. So he met the High Command with an order of his own, to "get off my ranch. This is my home, and I aim to keep it my home."

But they came back, the warriors, showing off the emblems of their rank, the rows of colored ribbons over their breast pockets, their shiny leather belts, brass buttons, the tailored cloth of their uniforms—and after many visits they found John Prather there to meet them, with a loaded rifle and a supply of ammunition at hand.

But he was weary with many years; he possessed not a fraction of the modern jaunty spirit that belonged to his persecutors—he was a pioneer. In spite of their mighty strength lone pioneers can match with a rifle so much and no more. Yet, he was the victor, the hero. They possessed his property, the wide ranges he rode from the days of his youth—but allowed him to live out his life in his home—and in his home he died.

Rita Hill of Shakespeare—

John Prather of the Sands of Alamogordo—

With such blood, heart, brain and sinew within its boundaries, Cowboy Riding Country will ride on forever.